1/26/19

To Phil,

You are a true
Superstar and
friend! More
importantly
You are
A
Solutions
Oriented
Leader!
your friend
Rick

ENDORSEMENTS

You'll love the direct, no-nonsense approach Rick Goodman uses throughout this book to share important leadership lessons that can be used immediately. The lessons and stories will do more than teach you to lead like a rock star. They will teach you how to create a team of rock stars!

—Shep Hyken
New York Times Bestselling Author of *The Amazement Revolution*

Rick's take on how you create a strong, productive, and successful team. This book explores conflict resolution, hiring, engagement, creating culture, communication, and collaboration. Read it to see how your own team-building efforts match up.

—Randy Gage
Author of the *New York Times* bestsellers
Risky Is the New Safe and *Mad Genius*

Dr. Rick Goodman is a no-nonsense genius who sees the world in a different way and tells it as it is. He promotes transparency, and I know Rick will shape the way you view your world.

—Mike Handcock
Global Speaking Fellow, Chairman of Rock Your Life,
and International Bestselling Author

Rick Goodman has distilled a lifetime of business experience into a must-read guidebook that will show you everything you need to know to be a successful leader.

—Bruce Turkel
Author, *All About Them*

The great achievers in history know that the secret to success is to find a problem and then solve it! The key is to grasp the power of finding the solution! Dr. Rick Goodman has tapped into a goldmine with his new book entitled, *The Solutions-Oriented Leader: Your Comprehensive Guide To Achieve World Class Results!* This book will give you power! If you want to achieve great results, then I highly recommend you get a copy of this book and read it, and then share it with everyone in your network. You will be glad you did! (And so will they!)

—Dr. Willie Jolley
Bestselling Author of *A Setback Is A Setup For A Comeback* and *An Attitude of Excellence*, Hall of Fame Speaker and Host of *The Willie Jolley Show* on Sirius XM Radio

The Solutions-Oriented Leader is a combination of common sense and extraordinary insight. Dr. Rick Goodman lays out a path for every leader at any stage to get better results quickly. This book is full of practical and achievable steps to become the leader you were destined to be!

—Barry Banther
Author of *A Leaders Gift, How to Earn the Right to Be Followed*

This is a fast-moving book loaded with great ideas that you can use immediately to set better goals, get more done, increase your income rapidly and feel terrific about yourself.

—Brian Tracy
New York Times Bestselling Author

If you are ready to take ownership and step-up your leadership skills, this book is packed with well-tested strategies for improving both management and leadership.

—Andrew Bryant, CSP
Global Leadership Coach
Author of *Self Leadership, How to Become a more Successful, Efficient and Effective Leader from the Inside Out*

Leaders are not born, they are made. Let Rick challenge you to be a better, more impactful leader. Read this book, but more importantly, put Rick's words into action and reap the rewards.

—Sam Silverstein
Author, *No More Excuses*
Past President, National Speakers Association

Few authors bring the depth of wisdom that Rick Goodman has brought to *The Solutions-Oriented Leader.* Taking the time to master even 10% of this material will put you on the inside track to saving countless hours with under-producing people, making you more effective so your company can make more money.

—Joel G. Block, CPA, CSP
Venture Capitalist and Hedge Fund Manager

In his practical and well-written book, *The Solutions-Oriented Leader,* Dr. Rick lays out the simple steps that you need to take to elevate your leadership to the next level. This is one of the best books I have read in a long time. I don't want to put it down!

—Elias Kanaris
Founder of the CEO Global Summit
President of the Global Speakers Federation (2018-2019)

Find out where you stand today as a
SOLUTIONS-ORIENTED LEADER.

TAKE THE FREE ASSESSMENT HERE
www.rickgoodman.com/solutions-oriented-leader-assessment/

THE
SOLUTIONS
ORIENTED
LEADER

DR. RICK GOODMAN

SOUND WISDOM
PO Box 310
Shippensburg, PA 17257-0310

For more information on publishing and distribution rights,
call 717-530-2122 or info@soundwisdom.com

Quantity Sales. Special discounts are available on quantity purchases by corporations, associations, and others. For details, contact the Sales Department at Sound Wisdom.

ISBN 13 HC: 978-1-64095-065-8

ISBN 13 TP: 978-1-64095-067-2

ISBN 13 eBook: 978-1-64095-066-5

For Worldwide Distribution, Printed in the U.S.A.

Cover design by Liza Santos

Library of Congress Cataloging-in-Publication Data

Names: Goodman, Rick, author.

Title: The solutions-oriented leader / Dr. Rick Goodman.

Description: Hollywood, Florida : Rick Goodman, [2018]

Identifiers: LCCN 2018032543 (print) | LCCN 2018053795 (ebook)
ISBN 9781640950665 (ebook) | ISBN 9781640950658
ISBN 9781640950658 (hardcover)

Subjects: LCSH: Transformational leadership.

Classification: LCC HD57.7 (ebook) | LCC HD57.7 .G665 2018 (print) | DDC
    658.4/092--dc23

LC record available at https://lccn.loc.gov/2018032543

1 2 3 4 5 6 / 22 21 20 19

To Alex and Jamie,

Watching you both grow into amazing adults who are making a positive contribution to our planet makes me so proud!

I love you more than the universe,

Dad

ACKNOWLEDGMENTS

To say this book has been a journey would be an understatement. It's been three years in the making and based on thirty years of my own personal success and failures.

I thank my unofficial Board of Directors for their support and feedback on this project:

Mitch Less, Will Ezell, Bruce Turkel, Randy Gage, Willie Jolley, Shep Hyken, Sam Silverstein, Lynn Rose, Werner Kwiatkowski, and of course, my amazing social media and editing team at Grammar Chic, Inc.: Amanda Clark, Kevin Clark, Josh Hurst, and Courtney Kulikowski—you always make me look great!

John Leone and Ralph Ledee—the lessons I've learned from your team have made a huge difference to companies around the world.

And to all the employees I have had in my formative years, thank you for the lessons I learned from you, which have enabled others to become rock stars!

CONTENTS

PREFACE

I believe that before we can become a solutions-oriented leader it's important to define just what that is! What are some of the traits and characteristics of a solutions-oriented leader and how do we begin our journey on the road to achieving world-class results?

Let's break it down and take the definitions of *solution, orient,* and *leadership* from the dictionary and see if we can learn something.

so·lu·tion

sə'lu-shən

noun: solution; plural noun: solutions

1. a means of solving a problem or dealing with a difficult situation

Synonyms: answer, result, resolution, way out, fix, panacea; key, formula, explanation, interpretation

o·ri·ent

'ôrē‚ənt

verb; orient; past tense: oriented

1. align or position

Synonyms: align, place, position, dispose

1. adjust or tailor (something) to specified circumstances or needs

2. guide someone in a specified direction

lead·er·ship

'lēdər,SHip

noun

1. the action of leading a group of people or an organization, "different styles of leadership"

Synonyms: guidance, direction, control, management, superintendence, supervision; organization, government

When we look at the definition of these words separately and then combine the definitions, we develop a set of all-encompassing traits for today's world-class solutions-oriented leader. To be more specific, a solutions-oriented leader can be an individual, corporation, association, private business, government or even colleges and universities can become solutions-oriented leaders.

Throughout this comprehensive guide to achieving world-class results, I share with you examples of how you can develop the skills to become a solutions-oriented leader who achieves world-class results as well!

INTRODUCTION

It's a funny thing about our modern world—communication has never been easier, yet connection has never seemed more elusive. Business leaders know this better than anyone. You have plenty of tools at your disposal to communicate with your employees—to talk *at* them and to get your point across. But how hard is it to sync your message with their needs—to actually *engage* them in their work as something collaborative, communal, and team-oriented? Now that's a challenge!

I wonder, though, if it's not a challenge that's worth tackling. In some ways it may be *the* most significant challenge that today's business leaders face! If you can position yourself to lead your team not just through commands and dictations but through *real engagement*, there is no end to what you can accomplish.

This book should also be considered a live case study. A few years ago, I had a discussion with the sales manager of a famous beer company where I had just conducted some training on negotiation skills. Subsequently, the management team was taking a leadership training program in San Juan, Puerto Rico. I was called in because the training the leadership team had engaged in while in Puerto Rico had missed the mark, and they wanted to see if I would be able to provide them with some solutions to help them improve the situation.

The problem was apparent to me, so I suggested some solutions to the sales manager and the country manager; however, the timing was not right to get started. I understood both the company's issues and the leadership team's issues because I had experienced all of them. And I was writing this book to share those solutions with leaders who truly wanted to transform their business and their organization by developing other leaders.

I contacted the country manager of the company in December to check in and see how things were going. He told me they still were not quite ready to bring me down to their headquarters to work with the team. He suggested we revisit the topic in August. I told him that six months was light years in business today and that he should assess the team sooner rather than later if he wanted to maintain and grow the business.

He thanked me and said he would think about it. Before we hung up, I told him about this book. Little did either one of us know that this book, my life, their company, and employees would never be the same again.

Within ten minutes of my phone call to the country manager, my phone rang—this time it was the sales manager who is a veteran in the beer distribution industry.

The first thing he said was, "Rick, my team sucks, I need to have lunch with you at Morton's restaurant on Monday."

The conversation was straight and to the point. I agreed to meet him Monday and I prepared for the meeting.

The day of the meeting I arrived early and waited for my client. The sales manager is one of the most passionate individuals I have ever met and has a heart as big as a house. It has been my experience, though, that in business, passion without control can have disastrous effects on a team.

I listened to his frustration for more than 90 minutes. At first, he wanted to fire everyone. The next minute he wanted to walk away from the business altogether.

The first thing I did was acknowledge his present situation. I understood it 100 percent. I had the same experience when I started my first business after graduating from chiropractic school. I had also witnessed it in many other corporations around the world.

The good news is that I had experienced both success and failure, so I knew I could provide solutions based on my past experience. The result would transform my client's employees into leaders and grow the business beyond his wildest expectations.

My Story: A Leader Without a Mission

I launched my first business more than 25 years ago. I was fresh out of chiropractic school and excited to build a big practice. I decided to surround myself with a team of superstars I would hand-pick to assist me in this journey. Perhaps like you, I had one big problem when I graduated—I had no training on how to hire people. I wasn't taught that in school.

What's more is that I had horrible leadership and communication skills. Frankly, I was just trying to graduate and did not understand the importance of acquiring those skills.

So, I hired some key players, including a front desk assistant. Unfortunately, things did not work out and I had to hire a new front desk assistant two days later. Over the next two years, I hired and fired more than 200 different front desk assistants. My patients couldn't help but provide commentary such as, "Doc, you must be tough to work for!" and "Who's the new front desk flavor of the month?"

One day, Bobbie, my current front desk assistant, walked into my office and said, "If you ever speak to me like that again, I'm out of here!" Well I can tell you one thing, to this day I cannot recall what the heck she was talking about or what I had said! However, her comment did make me realize that going through 200-plus front desk assistants in two years meant there was a problem.

The Problem Wasn't My Team—It Was Me!

I recognized that my team couldn't perform because it was lacking key qualities that any group needs in order to thrive. Qualities like communication, engagement, and leadership—just to name a few. And those qualities had to start with me.

The first thing I needed to do was find a mentor. I had to connect with some great leaders who had built outstanding teams and retained their employees for years. I figured they must have some "secret sauce" that enabled them to engage their employees and build multimillion dollar businesses, while also creating a culture of effective team members in a happy and productive work environment.

I made this my mission. I needed to discover what made high performers successful! Over the next two years, I traveled around the world and spent time learning from top leaders, CEOs, and entrepreneurs who had been responsible for creating and developing successful multimillion dollar businesses through a variety of business models and work environments. They shared with me their secret sauce—the stuff that made them winners and their employees exceptional team members!

For the past two decades, I've been implementing the lessons I learned to build superstar teams for Fortune 500 companies, the five branches of the Armed Forces, professional athletes, and Super Bowl championship teams. I've shared these lessons with audiences around the world, while delivering keynote speeches, breakout sessions, and facilitating "Transformational Roundtables" with spectacular results!

Now, I'm excited to share the wisdom I have gained through this journey and have implemented with great success! I am giving you the secret sauce that successful leaders have been using for years so you can transform your team into rock stars too!

When the leader improves, the team improves! This is the story of how transformational leadership and solutions-oriented principles will increase productivity and improve employee engagement and retention while creating a happy work environment.

Chapter 1

SUCCESS
BEGINS WITH YOU

**All Real Leaders
Exceed Their Job Descriptions!**

Are You the Problem or the Solution?

No matter what you say and no matter what you do, success ultimately begins with you! In order for me to begin my journey and for you to begin your own, understanding this principle is the starting point for developing excellent team members.

The good news is once you understand this you will be in control of your destiny. A number of years ago, on my birthday, which is October 6, I was reading the horoscope in the *New York Post*. This has been my personal ritual for more than thirty years. This time it was different, my life had taken an incredible turn when my wife of ten years, Jackie Klein Goodman, passed away after battling cancer. I had to make some life decisions, some easy and some more difficult.

My 50th birthday horoscope was a life-changing and profound statement. I actually had it framed and hung it in my bathroom. I look at it every day as a reminder of who really is in control of our destiny!

"If you want more freedom, then it's up to you to take it. No one is going to hand it to you on the plate. What is it that YOU want to do with your life? Then get on and do it, the only permission you need is your own!"

—New York Post, October 6, 2013

This quote spoke to me in many ways, especially when it was time to decide what was really important about being a leader, making my mark on the planet, and leaving a positive leadership and life legacy. I decided to look at things a little bit differently.

I heard about a goal-setting technique that many leaders used; the idea behind it was writing your own obituary. Think about what you would want people to say about you after you have left the planet. This seemed like a perfectly good idea to apply to leadership and what you want people to say about you as a leader after your professional business career is finished. I call this the *Leadership Epitaph*.

Your Leadership Epitaph

Try imagining this scenario, you've been a boss for more than 20 years, managing many employees in different positions throughout your career. You walk into a busy restaurant and suddenly look over and see one of your former employees. A few minutes later when you turn around, that person is whispering to friends. You imagine they're talking about you.

At this time, you're thinking about their conversation. The former employee gestures toward you, "You see that person over there? That used to be my boss."

"Oh really? A good boss or bad boss?"

Now here are my questions for *you*:

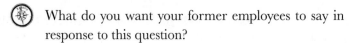 What do you want your former employees to say in response to this question?

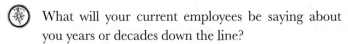 What will your current employees be saying about you years or decades down the line?

Will they remember you at all?

And if they pass you on the street, will their immediate recollections of you be fond and admiring—or negative?

This is your starting point for leadership self-evaluation. What really do you want? To be an excellent leader? Or to be a boss? We will discuss the difference later.

The leadership epitaph is the need for leaders to think about how they'll be remembered, and what that might mean for the way they lead their team right now, which contributes to their legacy in the future.

There are a couple of different dimensions to the leadership epitaph. There is the broader sense of what your tenure as a leader will ultimately mean to the company. Will you be remembered as the executive who created new jobs, expanded profits, and helped the company soar to new heights? Or will you be remembered as the person who was in charge during a period of major layoffs and losses?

Frankly, I think most employees will remember you less for the big picture stuff and more for the day-to-day. Do you lead by inspiring your employees—or yelling at them? Are you open to their feedback? Do you make them feel valued? Do you allow them to have their voices heard?

Do you empower your employees to be productive and *happy* in their work life?

These are the things your employees will remember. These are the things that will one day comprise your leadership epitaph. These are the things that I began to work on immediately in order to build my team and reach all of our goals. I encourage you to do the same. When I began my study of successful leaders, the one common denominator that I noticed was that *all real leaders go beyond their job descriptions!*

All Real Leaders Exceed Their Job Descriptions!

This brings me to an individual I admire because he brings out the best in everyone around him while remaining focused on his vision. He is truly a solutions-oriented leader who has not only exceeded his job description, he has also written a job description through his deeds and career for all to admire! Because of this, his leadership epitaph has already been written and it continues to grow daily.

Dr. Nido Qubein is an American Lebanese-Jordanian business-man, motivational speaker, and has been the president of High Point University in North Carolina since 2005. Dr. Qubein's background is impressive; however, his hard work and dedication to leading and developing solutions is what sets him apart from many in his field.

What makes him special is he never has forgotten his roots and always gives back more than is received. After graduating from High Point University in 1970, he went on to the University of North Carolina in Greensboro to earn his Master of Science in Business Education degree and returned in 2009 as he was awarded an hon-orary Doctor of Letters and Humanity.

More importantly a leader leaves an epitaph by taking action and developing solutions to problems that can stand the test of time! In 2005, High Point University was only 92 acres and landlocked to the total undergraduate enrollment of 1,450 students. The uni-versity's operating budget was only $38 million with approximately 100 faculty members. In 2017, High Point University undergradu-ate enrollment reached 5,000 students, a 245 percent growth; had a 203 percent increase in full-time faculty. The buildings on campus went from 22 to 112 with an over 409 percent growth; the operating and capital budget increased to $290 million, a 663 percent increase.

With the creation of new schools, majors, and courses, Dr. Qubein created a remarkable variety of learning opportunities for the students to embark on a new world and also become solutions-oriented leaders. High Point University's rankings soared from number 17 in 2005 to number one. The university was named the #1 regional college in the South for 2019, for the seventh consecutive year in "America's Best Colleges" by *U.S. News & World Report*. High Point was also recognized in "America's Best Colleges" as the number one most innovative, regional college in the South for making the most innovative improvements in terms of curriculum, faculty, students, campus life, technology, or facilities.

When we talk about what it takes to be a solutions-oriented leader who wants to make a difference in the world and leave a leadership epitaph to be proud of, Dr. Nido Qubein is an excellent example to model!

In the workplace, we tend to define ourselves according to job titles and descriptions. Our title establishes what we do, what we're in charge of, what our responsibilities are—and what's outside our obligation. Our job title defines what we need to do and what's frankly not our concern; it lets us know when we are fulfilling our obligations and, perhaps, when we are truly going the extra mile.

As I have studied successful leaders over the past thirty years, one of the common denominators is that they all exceed their job descriptions. In fact, many of them create their own job descriptions by going the extra mile in doing whatever it takes to get the job done and complete the goals and objectives of the organization.

So, what would happen if you didn't have a job description? What if you arrived at work one day and there was no longer any hierarchy, no way in which the members of your team were categorized? Would it be disastrous? Would it mean that work would grind to a standstill—or would people step up to do whatever it took for the team to succeed, regardless of whether it was truly "their responsibility" or not?

I'm not saying this is how things should be. Job titles and hierarchies serve useful functions in coordinating the office and facilitating delegation and project management.

However, your response to this hypothetical scenario may be telling. It may speak volumes about your propensity for real leadership.

Real leadership means understanding your job description, and the job descriptions of everyone on your team—but it also means not being *bound* by those descriptions.

Leadership isn't about doing only what is part of your job description. It's about doing anything and everything you can do to elevate your team members to a place where they can succeed, and about ensuring that everyone is working together toward meeting the team's goals.

Real leaders know that job descriptions can be helpful, but they don't tell the full story of your team members and their unique talents.

You may have someone whose job title technically involves sales and customer service—but what if that person also happens to be an extraordinarily gifted writer? Allowing that team member to write some company blog posts will be a boon to the entire team, and it will also help that team member feel respected, affirmed, and appreciated. It's a win for all, but to tap into that potential you have to know your team members beyond just their job titles.

And by the way, you also need to know your own strengths and weaknesses beyond whatever your job description entails. Leaders who are willing to earnestly assess and appraise themselves and to know where to be hands-on and where to delegate separate themselves from the rest of the pack and quickly develop followers.

This may mean coloring outside the lines of your official, formal job description—and if it does, then so be it.

Leadership means understanding your team, its members, and its goals—including, but not limited to, the titles that people hold. One technique I use to determine what my employees are doing is to have them write their own job descriptions.

This has allowed me to discover if my employees were on the right path and fulfilling their goals and objectives. It also gave me the opportunity to expand the parameters of their job, to focus on the highest and best use of their talents to reach their full potential in addition to reaching the company's goals.

If you're like me when you were in school, there were many leadership courses offered. In fact, it might've even been your belief that the best leaders were the loudest individuals in class. I've also met many people who thought that people had to be extroverts to be effective leaders.

When I started on my journey studying leadership success, I found a great discrepancy with my belief system. It was based on many false references within our culture. The fact of the matter is, though, from my experience and research, introverts make great leaders!

How Introverts Make Great Leaders

Unfortunately, it has been my experience that we live in a culture that closely links *extroversion* with *leadership*. Now, I'm a bit of an extrovert myself—but nevertheless, I have to say, as an international keynote speaker and leadership coach, that some of the *best*, most effective leaders I've seen have been introverts by nature. When we assume that *brashness* and *loudness* go hand in hand with decisiveness, we do so at our own peril.

One of the main things that holds introverts back, I think, is the perception that those who are quiet, even shy, cannot make commanding figures. That misconception keeps many introverts from reaching their true leadership potential, but it doesn't have to.

Consider the following four tips that you can use if you are an introvert to break through those perceptions and turn your introversion into an *asset*, not a liability.

1. **Remember that listening—not talking—is the mark of a really engaging leader.** The best leaders aren't necessarily the ones who talk the most. Often, they're the ones who actively listen, truly engaging with team members, colleagues, and customers before offering solutions. Introverts tend to be well-poised with their active listening skills.

2. **Remain calm during times of crisis.** When things get rocky, brash and loquacious, leaders can often fly off the handle—but introverts can be the voice of reason. Use that to your advantage! Seize crises as opportunities to provide stable, steady leadership.

3. **Force yourself out of your comfort zone.** You may not have much interest in making small talk or delivering big speeches—and to an extent, that's fine. But there's a case to be made for playing to your strengths.

Sometimes you have to push yourself a bit; that's the only way you'll ever grow as a leader.

4. **Allow yourself some quiet time.** Introverts need a little space to breathe, to recharge their batteries—and that's fine! Take 15 minutes each morning to be alone, to be quiet, and to give yourself some space before you tackle the challenges of the day.

By following these four tips, I believe that *any* leader, even an introvert, can break down the misconceptions and show real leadership skills. There is also another factor that leaders need to consider when starting on our journey toward success.

I'm talking about the way we handle situations and perceptions based on our past experiences. How we respond or how we react has a direct relation to our emotional intelligence (EQ).

Why Your EQ Matters as a Leader

Do you think a high IQ is a guarantee of business success? Think again! Today's leaders know that brains alone aren't enough to build a team or establish it for success.

Emotional engagement is just as important. This is where the concept of *emotional intelligence*—or EQ—comes into play in your success as a leader.

Maybe you're familiar with EQ. Basically, it refers to your ability to perceive and identify emotions in the workplace and in your relationships with others. It means being attuned to the emotions of the people around you, but also to your *own* emotions—and making your decisions accordingly. Many leaders I have worked with over the years have been highly skillful and intelligent, yet they couldn't control their emotions. Consequently, they had great difficulty getting others on board to back the missions and goals of the leader.

Emotional intelligence is a good predictor of your success in fostering relationships and forging strong teams. It's a concept worth learning more about, and an aptitude that's worth developing. Let me share with you what my studies have revealed.

EQ can help you cultivate employee engagement and retention. Today's employees don't merely want good salaries and benefits. They want a sense of belonging. They want a sense of social contact. If you can respond to the emotional cues of your employees and provide them with the sense that they are valued members of a true team, that can help you in both recruitment and retention.

Leaders with high EQ better understand how their employees derive satisfaction. Different people define *failure* and *success* in different ways and have different factors that motivate their workplace performance. Having EQ will help you identify these specific drivers for each employee and build a workplace dynamic that provides everyone with necessary motivators.

EQ can assist in team building, too. How do you get your people to collaborate? How do you structure a team that allows *everyone* to play to their unique strengths? EQ helps you to answer these questions and to build a team that works cohesively.

Finally, EQ can help identify your employees' management styles. How should you "handle" one employee compared to another, and which manager would make the best mentor for a given team member? These are the kinds of preferential questions that high EQ can help you answer.

As a leadership speaker, I meet countless executives and managers who are looking for the secret sauce—the competitive edge to take their team-building prowess to the next level. I'm telling you here that EQ is a big part of that sauce.

The good news is that there are many ways you can improve your emotional intelligence. The keys are accountability, self-assessment, a desire to improve, and the ability to recognize what you need to take responsibility and inspire others. Once you do that, you will know you that you are inspiring your team by paying attention to the seven traits of inspiring leaders.

Seven Traits of Inspiring Leaders

My first book, *Living a Championship Life: A Game Plan for Success,* contained a quote of mine that I live by. Located on the first page, it reads: "Leaders motivate and inspire—they relentlessly create the vision and set strategies for ACTION. Their ultimate gift is not to have followers, but to develop many other leaders."

Of course, you may be asking yourself, *Am I a great leader? Do I have the hallmarks of what it takes to be truly inspirational?*

A self-inventory is necessary to know for sure. However, to help you gauge your own leadership capacity, there is one thing I have noticed on my journey to success when studying some of the greatest leaders in business and in sports. There are specific signs, or traits, that you can look for to determine if you're inspiring your team or just hoping for the best.

I have identified seven traits of inspiring leaders during my personal journey to improve my own leadership skills to retain my employees and achieve the maximum productivity and happiness quotient we can have in our business. The list of seven traits follow:

1. **Perfecting a sense of purpose beyond your own success.** Wanting to achieve great things on your own terms hardly makes you a leader. No, leaders are folks who measure their own success by the success of others; they see it as their mission and purpose to help their team members thrive. If your purpose is to empower, you may be an inspiring leader!

2. **Approachable.** Do your team members feel comfortable approaching you with questions, concerns, or feedback—or do they tremble at the very thought of entering your office? If you're intimidating rather than approachable, that's a problem.

3. **Open-minded.** Great leaders are open to whatever works, even if it's not their own idea. Do you actively court solutions and suggestions from your team members—and implement the ones you think will work? Inspiring leaders do.

4. **Candid and constructive.** Inspiring leaders give the gift of feedback. If your team members actually accept your constructive feedback and make changes to their performance, that shows their respect for you, and that you're trying to help them improve.

The Solutions-Oriented Leader

5. **Treating your employees with equality.** Favoritism and inspiration do not work together. If your employees feel like you prefer some of them over others, that ultimately reflects badly on your leadership style.

6. **Being grateful.** Inspiring leaders are thankful for the efforts of their team—and they're not afraid to say so.

7. **Focus on your team.** If you're happy to give credit to team members, rather than hog it all for yourself, then you definitely have some inspiring leadership traits!

Take stock of yourself and use these points to determine how inspiring a leader you are already—you may even surprise yourself! Remember one thing, *teams go where you go!*

Your team will always take on the attitude and traits of its leader. My good friend, branding expert and frequent Fox TV Business personality Bruce Turkel, wrote a book titled *All About Them: Grow Your Business by Focusing on Others.* If we are to lead people, we have to focus on people first in order to be truly inspiring.

I have a saying, *"If you give to get, you're even. If you give expecting nothing in return, you're ahead of the game!"*

Success begins with you; so if you want to succeed as a solutions-oriented leader and turn your team into future leaders, focus on how you can support your team to achieve their goals and you'll achieve yours at the same time.

Chapter 2

ATTITUDE
IS EVERYTHING

Harness the Power of Positive Thinking.

I grew up in a home where my dad worked long hours and rarely came home until late at night. He certainly was not a world-class communicator; in fact, most of what I remember was pretty negative. I was told that I would fail and not achieve goals and expectations. I was not given support and affirmation.

I started to read self-help books and listen to audio recordings about maintaining a positive attitude. It took many years for me to reprogram my brain for success and it all started with self-affirmation. There is truly a power in what you say to yourself each morning because the brain does know the difference between what is actually happening and what is vividly imagined in great detail. Self-affirmation will make you think correctly about yourself.

Of course the old saying, "Sticks and stones may break my bones, but words will never hurt me," isn't really true. Words have power, and when they are wielded carelessly, they actually can hurt. In both your personal and professional relationships, the words you choose and the tone you take can shape the way other people feel— about you and about themselves.

Chances are, you know this truth from personal experience.

Perhaps someone said something thoughtless to you, and it really hurt. It caused you to lose some of your confidence or self-esteem. At the same time, people who speak carelessly can also do damage to themselves; perhaps someone says something rude to you and you simply lose your respect for them, finding it difficult to look past their haphazard remarks.

As a leader, the way you talk to your team members can have a dramatic impact on the way your team functions, and ultimately on the very way in which your company works. Here's something that's just as important, though, and even harder to implement: The way you talk to *yourself* also has huge ramifications and can make or break you in terms of everyday success.

That's why I think it's so important to start each day right—looking in the mirror and speaking a few words of affirmation to yourself. These don't have to be over the top; simply remind yourself that you are capable, that you are hardworking, and that you have what it takes to succeed. Build up your own confidence with some positive self-talk.

By no means is this a silly or nebulous exercise.

Psychologists agree that the way you speak to yourself can shape your attitudes and your actions throughout the day. Speaking positively to yourself pushes your subconscious to step up, take action, and spur you toward success—whereas speaking negatively to yourself will only suppress your potential.

Getting into the habit of self-affirmation can have other positive effects, too. For one thing, it will build within you a meaningful routine of affirmation. You'll find yourself speaking negative thoughts—*I can't do this, I'm going to fail,* etc.—much less frequently. You can shake off those confidence-killers once and for all.

Self-affirmation also helps you stay *focused*. It reminds you each and every day of what your purpose is, what you're trying to achieve, and how you're going to achieve it.

Speak powerful words into your own life—and watch how that confidence overflows into your daily activities, and even into the way you speak to others. I believe self-affirmation is one of the cornerstones for our success in business and in life!

For the past thirty years I have been using an affirmation that I received from a mentor of mine. I changed it slightly and applied it to my own life, and you can do the same. Apply the following affirmation to your situation and read it every day.

After thirty days, evaluate what type of days you have had since beginning this ritual. I have been sharing this affirmation with audiences around the world and attendees have written to tell me how it's made a positive difference in their lives. I know it will make a difference in your life as well.

You can also download my affirmation from this link: https://www.rickgoodman.com/morning-affirmation/ and feel free to share with others.

Morning Affirmation

I am a healthy, vital, active, happy and successful human being.

I affirm today that all tissues and organs in my body are functioning perfectly and that is the way it's supposed to be.

I am more relaxed than ever because I choose peaceful loving thoughts and release my fears, worries and anxieties.

Tension is gone because I am creating an atmosphere of ease and confidence.

My mind is uncluttered because I have set specific goals and planned action steps for their accomplishment.

I feel better now.

Nature uses the food that I eat and the air that I breathe, the water that I drink, and the rest that I get to rebuild, repair, and revitalize me for the future.

Radiant energy flows through me.

I also affirm today that money is plentiful and in abundant supply.

This money flows freely and constantly into my life as I render loving service to all mankind.

This morning affirmation is the first step. Now let's look at other ways we can attract positivity into our lives.

How to Harness the Power of Positive Thinking

It's not a shock or a surprise that people who have a positive outlook, who affirm themselves every morning, who visualize success and believe they can attain it tend to be the people who do the best, both in life and in business.

Positive thinking is about more than improving your attitude. It's about enhancing your ability to achieve. It's about expanding your capacity for success, however you may define the term. It's about proactively removing negativity from your field of vision so that you can be singularly focused on getting positive results in your professional life.

But how? How can positive thinking be not merely understood, but actually embraced?

I have a number of real-world tips that you can implement today that will help you to harness the power of positive thinking and keep some of the negative influences at bay. Each will help you keep focused on your goals and objectives and develop your exceptional team.

 Start to surround yourself with people who think positively. If you spend all day hobnobbing with complainers, don't be surprised when your own attitude takes a hit. Instead, try to find friends and family members who will offer you affirmation and enthusiasm. Allow yourself to bask in their positivity!

Express gratitude. Everyone has things in life for which we should be thankful. Take time each day to articulate what you're most thankful for and voice your gratitude to the people who deserve it. Saying *thank you* will transform your heart and mind.

Give. Rather than doubt your ability to make the lives of others better, be adamant about giving where you can—even if it's just giving some advice. Giving is a great way to orient yourself toward a more positive way of thinking.

Visualize success. What does success look like for you? What will it feel like when you meet your goals? Take some time each day to think about what success looks like. Visualize yourself achieving it. Make success feel more *real* and attainable to you. Remember, everyone is different; what means success to one person could mean failure to another, so get focused!

Be quiet. Spend a few minutes each morning just being quiet and alone—either meditating or simply doing some breathing exercises. Starting your day with a sense of calm can go a long way toward maintaining positivity through the rest of it.

Harness the *power of positive thinking* today and see how it transforms your mindset and your career, because the science is in and positive motivation really works!

Science Proves that
Positive Motivation Really Works

Today more than ever it's important to make sure we have correct information about leadership and employee engagement and that it is supported by research and statistics.

When it comes to motivating your employees, are you the good cop or the bad cop? Or to put it another way, do you tend to rely on the carrot or the stick?

For a long time, there has been disagreement over how best to engage and inspire a team—and while positivity has become increasingly favored, there's still a sense that it's really just a matter of subjective, personal opinion.

I'm here to tell you that's not the case. There is a science behind positive motivation.

In fact, there is scientific research that confirms the supremacy of positive motivation and you can read all about it in an article titled "From Scientific Research Come 6 Moves You Can Make to Boost Office Productivity" written by Moe Kittaneh in the June 2018 issue of *Entrepreneur* magazine.

According to the article, which cites a *Harvard Business Review* study, "Positive reinforcement actually motivates employees better than punishment. Not only is it more effective at motivating change, but it's also less damaging to the employer-employee relationship."

And it makes sense, right? In an environment where bosses *punish* rather than *praise*, it's only natural that the employees feel less trusted or valued.

Different Forms of Positive Motivation

Now, it's important to be clear that when I talk about positive motivation, I'm not merely suggesting that you give VISA gift cards to every employee who produces good work. Perhaps there is a time and a place for that sort of thing, but it's important to give other, equally valuable (but more budget-friendly) forms of positive motivation.

Continually reminding your employees of the big picture and their role within it—the company's goals, and how their job contributes to that goal—is *essential* and doesn't cost you anything.

Providing each team member with a sense of purpose, and a method for using their strengths in a way that moves the team toward the goalpost, is a must.

And allowing employees opportunities to learn, develop, and grow—showing that you're invested in their futures—is a powerful form of positivity.

There are many ways you can be the *good* cop to your employees. And if science is to be believed, you'll get much better results that way than you would otherwise. This approach leads into your company culture and how you can apply these principals to build a positivity.

Your Company Culture: Building and Maintaining Positivity

You can't force people to be happy—least of all your employees. What you *can* do, however, is create a workplace culture that promotes positivity.

As mentioned earlier, promoting positivity is a worthwhile undertaking, and for a variety of reasons. The first is that a positive workplace tends to breed positive people—and when your employees have positive energy, they tend to be more productive, more energetic, and more engaged.

That positivity spreads to customers, too. Have you ever done business with a company where the employees were *exceedingly* cheerful and kind? It probably made an impact on you. It probably made you glad to be doing business with them.

Every day more and more companies are investing millions of dollars in training their employees with tools and techniques on how they can better engage with their customers.

Instilling positivity in your company culture should be a top priority. Many companies ask me how this can be accomplished.

Let me offer a few recommendations about how you can bring and build positivity into your workplace culture. One of the places I always start is with the lesson that I learned in the book *The 7 Habits of Highly Effective People* by Stephen Covey—begin with the end in mind.

Begin with the End in Mind

This lesson—beginning with the end in mind—is where I start all projects in my life, because if you don't know what you want in life, you're never going to get it!

 Choose the kind of business you want to have. Ask yourself, *When an employee leaves my company, how will that person remember it? As a happy place, or as an oppressive one?*

Consider what kind of legacy you want to leave with your employees and make that your guiding concept. That's why you write your leadership epitaph.

 Hire positive people. Bringing positive people onto your team is paramount. Does a prospective employee complain about his or her current boss during the interview? That kind of attitude isn't going to change when they join your team. Hire smartly and be tuned-in for positive outlooks. We will discuss hiring and retaining great employees later on in the book.

 Encourage feedback—and listen to it. Encourage your employees to come to you with suggestions for improvement—and be grateful for whatever feedback you receive. You don't have to implement every suggestion made, but do really listen and respect the person offering it. Leaders who have an open-door policy and are transparent with their employees tend to build a following and a family culture where motivation is second nature.

 Give recognition where recognition is due. Don't hesitate to provide public praise or rewards for team members who do exemplary work. Show your appreciation for the people who work for you. I like to say, "Catch people doing the right thing and you will reinforce that behavior." Another great way of recognizing people is through a company newsletter that helps to build a culture of family while recognizing your employees on a periodic basis. This can also be used to promote your business and company culture to your existing and future clients.

Provide a sense of purpose. The enemy of positivity isn't necessarily negativity, but rather *aimlessness*. You can combat this by making sure all your employees know what your vision is, and how they play a part in achieving it. Continually reinforce your mission and vision for the company with communication on a daily basis, so they feel as if they are part of the plan.

These are just a few recommendations to consider.

However, there's another way to build a great sense of positivity in your culture, enhance the self-esteem of your employees, and assist others in the community—philanthropy.

The natural progression of building a culture of positivity and caring was to motivate my team through the use of philanthropy. Each year I created projects that would help others who were less fortunate than we were. The change in our team attitude following these events was always amazing!

Philanthropy Motivates and Builds Your Team

Again, let's visit High Point University and Dr. Nido Qubein who has set an example for all to follow. No this is not a paid advertisement for Dr. Qubein and HPU, it's simply an opportunity to learn and model a great example of what can be done when your goal is to become a solutions-oriented leader.

Dr. Qubein's focus is on philanthropy; he understands that it can be the great game changer in any transformation—whether a business or your own personal transformation. He lives by William Barclay's mantra, "Always give without remembering; always receive without forgetting."

In fact, the National Speakers Association named its philanthropy of the year award for Dr. Qubein. The city of High Point in North Carolina named him philanthropist of the year, as did the Triad Association of Fundraising Executives. The Qubein Foundation has awarded hundreds of scholarships to students across North Carolina and the country.

So you may ask, how does this build my team? It's pretty simple—actions always speak louder than words, and if you want people to follow you, to really get behind you, to make a difference, you can only achieve this with deeds and actions. Words won't cut it!

Dr. Qubein did exactly that. *The Chronicle of Higher Education Almanac,* April 19, 2016, noted that Dr. Qubein was the third-highest donor university president from 2006-2016 when he committed $10 million of his own money to High Point University. Now that's putting your money where your mouth is and leading by example!

In 2004, High Point University's charity of choice, United Way Giving, received $28,000 in charitable giving by High Point University. That number has increased by 759 percent to $240,580 in charitable giving, a number that the whole university—alumni, faculty, students, and parents—can be proud of!

In addition, because of the philanthropic nature of the president and the university as a whole getting behind the vision and mission of its president, it has built a legacy that will endure and stand the test of time. High Point University will continue to develop the most innovative programs in the country because they now have the resources to accomplish this based on their giving at High Point, more than their receiving.

Now with gifts and pledges since 2005 totaling more than $300 million, including ten gifts of $10 million or more, the university is able to build new facilities to accommodate residential students and new athletic buildings to support 16 NCAA Division I sports teams and expand the campus from 92 acres to 430 acres. If this doesn't convince you about the power that philanthropy has when building your team, your company, and your life, I don't know what will!

In an effort to pad their culture and motivate employees, many companies spring for superficial trappings—ping-pong tables, casual dress Fridays, fridges stocked with exciting snacks. In fact, we do that at our company too!

These things are fine, but the appeal is fleeting. Once the novelty wears off, the motivational power is diminished.

But what if I told you there was a motivational technique that offers much more lasting value? Something that helps others and builds your employees' self-image at the same time. Would you be interested?

I'm talking about philanthropy—or to be more politically correct, corporate social responsibility. Align your company with a cause that allows your employees to feel like they are adding value to the world—that they and your company are part of something bigger, and something good.

This sense of mission, of doing good in the world, can keep employees engaged with their work and optimistic about the impact they are making. That's what makes it such a valuable addition to your company culture.

One of the keys to this strategy is to get your employees to decide which important charitable causes they want to be involved with and support. This is a must because you want to have buy-in from all of your employees. If it's a charity that they cannot get behind, it may make the goal more difficult to accomplish.

Three specific benefits of adopting a culture of philanthropy:

1. **Philanthropy leads to happiness.** There's something to be said for a *happy employee base!* Philanthropic giving stimulates the brain and causes the release of endorphins; there is true, physiological happiness generated, which in turn leads to lower turnover and higher productivity.

2. **Your team will bond.** A culture of philanthropy fosters a sense of camaraderie; everyone is working together and has a common objective, which can increase your team's sense of cohesion. This impacts all levels of your business.

3. **It's fulfilling.** Your employees may not feel totally, inwardly satisfied by meeting big sales goals—at least, not forever. But active kindness and compassion can go a long way toward boosting that sense of fulfillment—and again, the result is lower turnover and *higher workplace satisfaction.*

Chapter 3

FOLLOW
THE LEADER

**Nobody Likes Following a Boss,
But Everyone Loves Following a Leader.**

Much has been written about the difference between a boss and a leader. In fact, there is no doubt in my mind that when I started out I was definitely a boss. I learned this from watching my dad because he was a boss and he was always telling people what to do.

Unfortunately, I had to figure this out the hard way after losing so many employees during my first two years in business. Remember, nobody likes following a boss, but everyone loves to follow the leader! The decision you make about being a boss or a leader will affect everything you do from your communication to your outcomes.

Let's take a look at what the difference is so that you can make an educated decision on which path you want to follow.

One thing you can do that is always helpful is to think about some of the best leaders you have had in your life.

They may have been at work or could have been a teacher or coach. Write down the traits that you believe make these people great leaders. Adopt the traits that really stick out in your mind and begin to make those traits your own.

Eventually you will have your own leadership style that will be formed based on what you learned, what you studied, and what you experienced.

Now let's take a look at some of the differences between a boss and a leader and then you can choose who you really want to be.

The Difference Between a Boss and a Leader

The words *leader* and *boss* may have pretty similar dictionary definitions—but in the business world, their practical distinctions are crucial.

Just think about their connotations. Most of us think of a boss as someone who makes demands, yells at us when we screw up, and ultimately has the power to fire us at will. A leader, meanwhile, is someone who inspires us, coaches us, rallies the team, and helps everybody move forward.

So, which are you? Consider some of the following traits of a leader versus a boss:

Leaders actually lead. By contrast, a boss rules, governs, and dictates. A boss may sit in his office all day hammering out policies and telling everyone else what to do—but a leader is right there in the fray with the rest of the team, guiding *everyone* in the right direction.

Leaders listen. Bosses are not known for their acceptance of feedback or openness toward collaboration. By contrast, a leader wants to hear what team members have to say and to engage them in the decision-making process. This does not mean that the leader is obligated to utilize the feedback given by employees; the ultimate goal is to be inclusive of everybody. People want to be listened to and heard, which is the cornerstone of effective communication.

Leaders empower. Bosses might throw their employees into a project without much training or guidance—leaving them fearful and insecure. Great leaders, meanwhile, do everything to prepare their team members and instill them with confidence in their own abilities and in the abilities of the team. When a team member fails to achieve an objective, a good leader will give them the tools to be more successful the next time.

Bosses intimidate. Leaders know better than to use fear as a tool for managing their team members. When an employee is intimidated it could have a paralyzing effect on the employee, which can decrease the person's productivity and limit the amount of engagement and motivation to buy-in to the company's goals and objectives.

 Bosses think of themselves as above other employees. This is the proverbial kiss of death for any business. In my experience, when people worked *for* me, they left me; when they started working *with* me, they stayed for years and years. A solutions-oriented leader is open to *constructive feedback* from team members and knows that there is always more to learn—even from lower ranking employees.

 Bosses yell at people. When bosses yell at someone in front of the team, they send a negative message to everybody: Watch out, it could happen to you next! Even your top employees will take offense to this type of communication and will support the employees who were yelled at. This is a very dangerous precedent and I've seen it backfire and destroy businesses. Good leaders ensure that their feedback is constructive and action-oriented—and that it is offered in private, not in front of the whole team. Speak to your employees like you speak to your mother and everything should be just fine.

 Bosses focus on hierarchies. Bosses have an attitude of, "I'm your boss and *I* tell *you* what to do." Leaders focus on relationships with an attitude of, "How can we improve and move forward *together?*"

For the past thirty years, I've been asking audiences this one specific question when presenting a keynote speech, "How many of you like to be told what to do? Please raise your hands." When I ask this question, there are only a few hands that are ever raised.

I know that when we were teenagers many of us thought, *I can't wait to get out of my parents' house. When I do, nobody's ever going to tell me what to do again!* In my humble opinion I think we're all children in big people's clothes. The fact is, even as an adult, when someone tells me what to do, my mind immediately goes to the thought, *You're not my mother. You're not going to tell me what to do. I'll show you!*

This thought process is based on past experiences and references a sort of fight or flight reflex. I know one thing after studying some of the most successful leaders in the world—there are a lot of people who are just like me, and maybe you are one of them!

The difference in attitude makes *all* the difference. So again the question is, which are you—a boss or a leader? If you choose to become a leader, there are six changes you can implement immediately to become more of a leader and less of a boss.

Six Ways to Become a Better Leader

If you've made the decision to become a better leader, to motivate your team and leave a legacy that you can be proud of, there are some changes you may need to make to your leadership style *today* that will point you in the direction you want to go.

1. **Learn to listen rather than bark orders.** My grand-mother always told me, "You have two ears and one mouth in order to listen twice as much as you speak!" This was fantastic advice given to me at 10 years of age. The next time you're tempted to issue a set of commands, stop yourself. Instead of commanding, call your team together for a discussion. Listen to what they have to say. Ask for advisement in the areas you feel weakest. Work together toward a solution, and then move forward.

2. **Find tools for motivating your employees rather than scaring them.** Provide metrics and data to your team members, showing them the impact they make and what their work means. Tell them that what they do is meaningful. Involve them in decision-making and invest in educating and training. Gamification is also a great way to get people involved since almost everyone likes to play games. This way you can accomplish goals and have fun at the same. Find whatever tools you can to motivate them rather than threatening or frightening them.

3. **Step away from micromanagement.** Don't try to control your team members. Just provide them with some basic guidance. Share a goal and some resources for meeting that goal and let your team take it from there. The fact of the matter is, you may find that people can do an even better job than you thought they could. The result—the development of future leaders who can help grow your company and have now grown themselves.

4. **Make sure your feedback is constructive.** If you yell
    at your team members or seek to embarrass or punish
    them, you're not a leader. It's as simple as that. Lead-
    ers provide constructive feedback to address problems,
    improve performance, empower people, and ultimately
    yield better results.

    I use a simple technique called *Like Best, Next Time*.
    When giving feedback I tell my employee what I like
    best and what I would do different next time and then I
    ask what the person likes best and what he or she would
    do different next time.

    Most people who make a mistake are already saying to
    themselves, *The next time I'm going to do this another way.* If
    I give them constructive criticism or feedback that they
    do not appreciate, they won't learn a lesson. Most peo-
    ple inherently have an idea of what they would do dif-
    ferently the next time; and when they fix it themselves,
    they never make the same mistake again. If I fix it for
    them, they'll continue to make the same mistake.

5. **Delegate.** To be a leader, you have to trust your team
    members to tackle projects on their own. Take some-
    thing that's on your plate and give it to an employee.
    That's the first step toward meaningful delegation. I
    like to use a technique I call *Check Back!* This is one of
    the best delegation techniques I have ever used. Like
    mentioned previously, most people don't want to be told
    what to do.

    So when I delegate tasks to employees, I present them
    with the task and then ask the question, "When can I
    check back with you?" The ball is now in their court;

now they have to commit to when they're going to get the job done and when I can check back with them.

The key to *Check Back* is that you must check back! If you don't, you will lose all credibility. There are so many times when people have been asked to drop everything they were working on to do something for the boss who claimed it was urgent. Sound familiar? Then when the task is complete, the boss never even used the work that was completed. I know what you were thinking, because I thought the same thing: *The next time I'm asked to do something, I'm not doing it!*

6. **Be generous in your praise.** Give credit where credit is due, and make sure your employees know that you notice and appreciate their hard work. Create recognition activities and employee of the month programs that stimulate positive behavior and workplace camaraderie.

Even though you may feel like more of a boss than a leader in the beginning, and you may not like it one bit, the good news is that change is possible. This is especially true if you implement some of these changes today and focus on becoming a solutions-oriented leader.

Leaders who haven't developed a culture of positivity will generally find something wrong in every situation. The leader who has developed a culture of positivity is generally what I like to call a solutions-oriented leader.

This type of leader has developed specific traits that lead to consistent success.

Five Traits of a Solutions-Oriented Leader

Everyone responds to problems in different ways. Some immediately start turning over the problem in their minds, perhaps looking for the reason the problem emerged or they seek out related problems that may not have dawned on them yet. But others look beyond the problem to the *solution*—immediately looking for ways to solve the issue and move forward.

There's probably room for both ways of thinking—but if you're in a position of leadership, your employees are going to look to you for answers. To a large extent, they need you to have solutions, not just theories about the problem itself.

So, developing a solutions-oriented approach to leadership is certainly commendable. The question is, how do you know when you get there? How do you know if you're truly a solutions-oriented leader? What are some steps you can take right now to become a solutions-oriented leader?

To become a solutions-oriented leader, there are five things you can do immediately do to get the ball rolling:

1. **Look at a problem and see the possible outcomes— the possible *future*.** If you allow yourself to become emotionally involved in a problem—getting your feelings hurt or growing resentful over it—then you're not really thinking about solutions. Don't dwell in the past; start building the future. It's important to hover above the problem so you can look down on it. When we are involved in things that are close to us or are right in front of us, we tend to have blind spots that prevent us from seeing the big picture and coming up with a successful

course of action. Successful leaders think and see the overall big picture and make plans for the future.

2. **Think systematically and strategically.** You're at Point A. You need to get to Point B. A solutions-oriented mind immediately starts thinking about methods to close the gap and make that change. Plan out step-by-step actions that you can take to achieve your goals. Begin with the end in mind!

3. **Be accountable, don't make excuses!** Solutions-oriented leaders simply don't make excuses. They don't care about whose fault it is so much as what can be done to make things right. They don't get involved in the blame game. They look forward and just fix the problem!

4. **Resist problem-oriented questions.** Some employees will inevitably ask, "Why did this happen?" The solutions-oriented leader doesn't focus on these types of questions because it's often a waste of time. Focus less on why and more on what do we do now? As mentioned previously, teams go where you go! The leader who focuses on problems attracts problems—and the leader who focuses on solutions attracts solutions. Keep your team focused on solution generation and that's what you will attract—turning your team into rock stars!

5. **Take a collaborative approach.** The solutions-oriented leader knows that the most important thing is to find a way forward—and the best way to do that is to pull the whole team together into brainstorming and collaboration. Many times I have observed a leader being too close to the problem to come up with a solution.

When a leader decides to take a collaborative approach, the results unfold rapidly, and the solution appears. That's why building a diverse team is so important and plays a major role in developing your team.

The next time a problem arises in your workplace, consider your response. See if you can find some ways to focus less on the issue itself and more on the possible *solution—while at the same time being aware of turning into a micromanager.*

A micromanager can immediately stop people from finding solutions. I have seen hundreds of cases of micromanaging leaders who have unenthusiastic and unmotivated teams that are looking for a way out so their true talents can be fully utilized and developed.

If you're a micromanager and your team isn't working to its maximum ability, I think I know why. Nobody likes a micromanager!

Are You a Micromanager?

As part of my leadership coaching, I often ask people, "What kind of leader do you most like to work for?" This can be a helpful way to get people to understand their own style, their own needs and preferences.

I've asked the question many times and to many people, and I've received a multitude of answers. There's one answer I've never received, though. I've never heard *anyone* say they wanted to work for a *micromanager.*

That's because, well, nobody likes micromanagers.

That kind of leadership style can have a corrosive impact on trust and positivity in your company culture. And yet, micromanagers do exist. In fact, it's not impossible that you're one of them. I was a micromanager until I learned how much it was hurting my team and my results!

Telltale Signs of a Micromanager

How can you tell if you are a micromanager? The following are some quintessential traits of micromanagers, and after reading each, you can decide for yourself how many of these fit your leadership style. If indeed you are a micromanager, it may be time to do some soul-searching, or even to invest in an executive coach to help you modify your leadership approach. This was one of the first steps I took on my road to building a team of leaders!

You may be a micromanager if:

 You obsess over control. You constantly need to know what everyone on your team is doing. You insist that everything be done your way, and you routinely return work that doesn't meet your particular standard. You *fear* the loss of control in your office. I have seen leaders who obsess over control, which delays the decision-making process and ultimately causes financial loss. Remember that FEAR stands for False Evidence Appearing Real! Most of the things we worry about never happen.

 You try to do everything all on your own. You ultimately think you can run a business as a one-person show. Unfortunately, in today's world there is just too much to accomplish in order to be successful in business and think that you can do it all on your own.

You believe that you alone have the best approach to every task...and that your employees don't have good ideas or alternative points of view that are worth considering. Everyone comes with a different experience based on our lifetime of references and lessons from the past. Leaders who are open to listening to the viewpoints of their team often find that the information they receive helps them to scale their business and streamline their processes.

You are constantly suspicious that people are wasting time and resources. You ask for detailed records of supply use, phone calls, etc. Leaders who major in minor things also have minor achievements. A happy team member is a productive team member. After all, don't you have anything better to do? Like grow your business and reach your goals!

You look for any excuse to schedule a meeting...no matter how unnecessary it may be. This could be the biggest sign of all! Are you bored? Meetings are only important if there is a specific goal and expected outcomes tied to an agenda. If not, don't have a meeting! Nobody likes meetings anyway.

You refuse to delegate. Or when you do delegate, you immediately start second-guessing your decision. The only way to grow people is by giving them responsibility and delegating to them tasks that are going to make them more efficient and grow their skill level. If you are refusing to delegate, you are refusing to grow your business and your people, and that's a losing proposition.

Begin by diagnosing yourself; and if you meet any of the criteria of a micromanager, well, it's a safe bet that you've already been diagnosed as such by members of your team. That said, you might want to rethink your approach to leadership and become less of a micromanager.

Consider this scenario. Your spouse, or significant other, asks you to get the salt from the cabinet. When you open the cabinet door to get the salt, you can't find it. Even though you are looking right where the salt is always kept, you can't see it. Then your spouse walks over, says, "It's right here in front of you," grabs it, and walks back to the table.

This is called a *scotoma*—another word for *blind spot*. It's important as we grow into our role as leaders that we pay attention to our leadership blind spots in order to strengthen our skills that need improvement, making us even better leaders.

Five Tips for Identifying Your Leadership Blind Spots

Like I said, it doesn't matter how great of a leader you become—how experienced, how deliberate, how much of an expert in your field. You're still going to have some weak areas—areas that need improvement.

Many leaders don't actually *recognize* these areas in themselves, which means they *don't* improve, and don't seek assistance when they really need it. These are leadership blind spots, but they don't have to be yours. It is possible to identify them and work toward improvements—making yourself a more robust and multitalented leader than ever.

Here are a few tips for avoiding this trap that stagnates the growth of your leadership skills, which ultimately affects the team.

1. **Find and conquer your leadership blind spots.** Tactfully ask other leaders and your mentors what they think *their* blind spots are. Help develop your own awareness of some of the most common leadership blind spots that are out there. You'll probably hear other executives list *communication* or *organization* or *delegation* as some of their top areas for improvement. Perhaps this can spur some introspection on your own part.

    Sometimes it's very helpful to survey and ask the question, "What don't you like to do as part of your job?" I find that what many leaders do not like to do are the areas in which they need to improve the most.

2. **Hire people who are different from you**—people who have different skill sets and areas of strength. Not only will this help relieve your own shortcomings, but will help you cover and protect against them from deterring progress and success. Building a diverse team gives leaders options they would never have without the diversity of thought and talent and skills. The diversity of experience in any team can be its greatest asset by a solutions-oriented leader—or even as a crutch to move forward if a boss lacks an open mind.

3. **Solicit feedback from your team members.** Make it clear that you value their comments, even constructive criticism, and invite them to "review" your leadership during their own annual employee reviews. One of the best traits any leader can have is transparency and a desire to grow. The leader who possesses these traits will

be secure with feedback from their team, which will lead to their own personal growth.

4. **Think about some of your own habits.** This can be a good way of identifying strengths and weaknesses. For instance, if you have a habit of arriving at meetings late, then perhaps organization is a weakness. And if you have a bad habit of stress eating, you may need to develop tools for stress management. It's always best to assess ourselves, but if you feel you need help with the assessment, find someone you trust who will be completely honest with you and then ask them to share their observations so you can improve as a leader and a person.

5. **Make a list of your strengths**—but consider how each can come with liabilities. For example, persuasive and commanding speakers sometimes have a hard time listening to others; those who are decisive and dedicated may struggle with delegation. Spend time thinking about the ways in which your leadership can be improved—that kind of self-awareness can be invaluable on your quest to improve as a solutions-oriented leader.

It's also been my experience in business that there are those leaders who tend to hoard information in order to stay in control. This is a big mistake in my opinion! The more a leader shares and collaborates with the team to achieve goals, the more effective that team will be in completing the task effectively.

The leader who understands this concept will create an amazing work environment that is highly productive, have an increased rate of employee retention, and experience happy and satisfied customers.

Collaboration is one of the cornerstones of leadership success. After all, *you can't do everything yourself!*

The Power of Collaboration

As a business leader, what do you think is your greatest resource? It's not anything monetary or physical; it's not your business plan or your posh office space. Your most precious resource is your *team*— each member offering a unique perspective and skillset from which you can cultivate and refine your business.

The question is, are you taking full advantage of this resource? Many leaders, frankly, do not. They sit in their offices and dictate their ideas rather than rolling up their sleeves, pulling up a chair, and getting down to the important work of *collaboration*.

Collaborating with your team members is the only real way to tap into their great ideas, to nurture their creativity, and to push *yourself* to be smarter, more effective, and more innovative.

In a word, collaboration is what real, solutions-oriented leaders do. It's how you show you're serious about building a stellar team and a successful business.

But what does a really *collaborative leader* look like? Here are some signs you should look for to determine if you're a collaborative leader:

 Collaborative leaders believe that power comes from a team working together as one—not just from one central authority figure.

 Collaborative leaders openly share information rather than hoarding it; information is a tool for the whole team to benefit from, not something to hold onto or to hoard.

Collaborative leaders are open to suggestions and give team members a voice for making their ideas known. They empower, rather than silence, and they recognize that anyone on the team can have great ideas—not just the leader or the business owner.

Collaborative leaders brainstorm solutions rather than dictating them.

Collaborative leaders are comfortable when roles and responsibilities evolve; they embrace fluidity rather than clinging to rigid structure. Collaborative leaders go beyond their job description!

Collaborative leaders are not stingy with the gift of their feedback. They endeavor to make feedback constructive. They are open to receiving feedback as well as dispensing it.

Collaboration is the hallmark of an effective team—and it doesn't come about by accident. It comes about only when the leader embraces, exemplifies, and encourages it—even in the face of workplace turmoil and change. The good news is that when you hire the right people, collaboration is much easier because like attracts like!

Chapter 4

LIKE ATTRACTS
LIKE

**Hiring Leaders or Developing Them...
It's Up To You!**

I truly believe that like attracts like. If we are being the best leaders we can be, we will attract the right employees. My motto is, *Hire Slow and Fire Fast, but Hire Smart!*

Team Building Begins with Smart Hiring

Here is the great paradox of team building—a great team is one in which the *group* is stronger than the sum of its members. At the same time, a team cannot succeed unless all of the individuals who comprise it are dedicated to the team's vision and to its success.

To put all of that another way—team building requires you to look at the big picture, but you can't neglect all of the individual parts—all of the individual gifts, talents, and attitudes that *paint* that big picture.

Team building requires group exercises, bonding, and communication—but also focus on each individual. As the leader of the team, you have to invest time in each member of your team, helping each person to develop the necessary skills and the right attitude for your team dynamic.

When should you begin this work of individual investment? *There's no time like now.* You should start as soon as possible, if you haven't already—and in fact, the work of assembling a strong team, comprised of strong individual players, begins not with your annual corporate retreat or your quarterly team-building exercise, but *during the hiring process*.

Yes, assembling your dream team means paying attention to the folks who interview with you and ensuring that you're hiring not just on the basis of their skills or their resume accomplishments, but also on the basis of how they fit into your team and complement your other players.

Some tips:

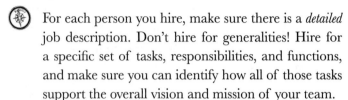

For each person you hire, make sure there is a *detailed* job description. Don't hire for generalities! Hire for a specific set of tasks, responsibilities, and functions, and make sure you can identify how all of those tasks support the overall vision and mission of your team.

Always look for complements. You don't build a good team by hiring a group of people who all act and think like each other. You also don't build a good team by hiring a group of people who all act and think *like you do*. Always hire for fresh perspectives and skillsets.

You don't want to hire solely on the basis of personality, but neither do you want to avoid thinking about personality. An applicant may have all the technical skills you need, but what if he or she simply won't mesh well with the other team members? Skills you can teach, but basic personality you can't—and a clash of personalities could prove disruptive to the team dynamic.

Don't be afraid to solicit input from your team! Ask what kind of player *they* think you need to hire—what skills are needed in the office, what personality traits to look for, and so forth.

Be clear in communicating your team's purpose and vision during the interview process. Make sure the applicant is on board with it, even *enthusiastic* about it. Don't wait until the onboarding process begins to talk about important, big-picture matters of company culture.

 Involve some of your team in the hiring process. After all, the individual being hired will most likely be working with the team member and it's also important to gauge the chemistry between new and existing employees.

Many of my challenges with employee turnover and retention were based on the fact that I hired the wrong people. Now is the time to look at some of the signs you should be aware of so that this doesn't happen to you.

How to Know if You're Hiring the Wrong People

Effective team building begins with smart hiring. It's important for any business to have policies and standards in place, ensuring the right people are hired—and if the wrong people are being hired, corrections are promptly made to the hiring process.

Of course, even the best recruiters and hiring managers misfire from time to time, bringing in an employee who simply does not fit with the company culture. When it happens habitually, though—well, that's a major warning sign that something is wrong in the hiring process.

So how do you know when the company is hiring the wrong people? What are some of the red flags to be aware of? The following warning signs are important to recognize:

 Your employees seem to know very little about the organization. If you have new hires who seem to know almost nothing about your company's vision and values, it's probably because of a faulty onboarding process—but it may also be because you've hired people who have done little or no research into the company, and thus have not made an educated decision about accepting a position in your organization.

- **Your employees have totally different values from yours.** Are you hiring for *fit*, as well as for skills? You may have candidates who have the right resume qualifications but don't have the same conception of success. That may have a corrosive effect on your team dynamic and company culture.

- **You and your employees have different concepts of work and life balance.** Do you expect your team members to work super-long days, or do you feel strongly that they need to punch out to recharge their batteries? If your opinion differs from that of your employees, it could be problematic.

- **Your employees are loners.** There's nothing wrong with hiring introverts, but if your employees simply refuse to be collaborative—well, that's going to make it hard to build a strong team!

- **You feel like you have to sell your business too hard.** You should seek employees who are enthusiastic to work with you, not those who have to be convinced!

- **You ignore your gut feeling during the hiring process.** You need to make sure your mind and your gut agree; if your gut is trying to tell you something, you're foolish to ignore it.

Bottom line: You want to hire the right people. You *need* to hire the right people. And that means knowing when you're hiring the wrong ones.

Now let's take a look at how culture fits into your recruiting process.

How to Use Culture When Recruiting

Millennials (people born between the early 1980s and the early 2000s) differ from previous generations in several respects. But I'd argue that the most *significant* is that they don't take jobs solely on the basis of benefits or even career advancement. Both of those aspects can be important, but more than anything else, young employees today want to align themselves with the right company *culture*. They want to be part of a business that complements their personal values and mission—a company they can respect.

If you want to attract the best young workers, it's important to turn your company culture into an asset—a selling point. But this isn't just about getting the best talents. It's about attracting talents who will *fit* within your organization and align with its purpose and objectives.

All that's well and good—but how exactly do you use your culture in the recruiting process? Let me provide just a few brief recommendations.

Recruiting with Your Company Culture

 Use Your Website: One thing I like is when company websites go into detail about the culture. This requires you to be *specific* and *transparent*. Saying, "Our team members work hard and play hard" doesn't really reveal anything. Talking about specific team-building activities, showcasing the ways in which meetings are run to give *all* team members their say…those are the kinds of details that can make your website a powerful showcase for your culture.

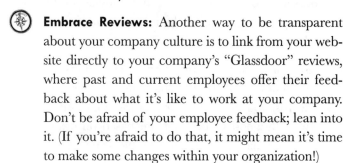

Embrace Reviews: Another way to be transparent about your company culture is to link from your website directly to your company's "Glassdoor" reviews, where past and current employees offer their feedback about what it's like to work at your company. Don't be afraid of your employee feedback; lean into it. (If you're afraid to do that, it might mean it's time to make some changes within your organization!)

Involve Your Team: You might also consider getting your whole team involved in the hiring process. As mentioned previously, rather than only the managers interviewing, have other employees who will be working with the new hire sit in and provide feedback. They can be really helpful in answering culture-related questions that new recruits might have.

Make culture an asset and be aware of any biases that you may have because that will impact the recruiting and hiring process also.

Are There Biases in Your Recruiting Practices?

No one wants to believe they are in any way prejudiced, but let's be honest, as human beings, we all have biases, opinions, and our own perceptions. As much as we might resist, these things can all cloud our judgment and impact our decision-making. That includes the decisions we make about hiring, firing, and recruitment.

As a leadership speaker, I talk to a lot of business owners and Human Resource managers, and I've become familiar with some of the most common hiring and recruitment biases. Before you defend yourself as being totally impartial, I invite you to give yourself a check-up while consulting the following brief list of common recruiting biases:

 Unfair extrapolations and assumptions. This is sometimes called the "halo/horn" bias—in other words, you just get a *vibe* that the applicant is either a really good or bad person, based on criteria that may be shaky at best. For example, you might subconsciously assume that the applicant who is well-dressed and physically attractive is a good worker; that the one with the annoying nail-biting habit isn't; or that the applicant with strong sales experience would also make a good sales manager, even though there's really nothing to back up any of those assumptions.

 Biases based on recent hiring trends. This bias can come in many forms. One of the most common: "The last three people we hired were *great*, so let's just hire some more!" Or, "The last person I hired with a degree from *this* school was horrible, so let's ignore people with a similar background."

 Biases relative to your current employees. If you go into a hiring process to replace your sales director, Marion, and begin with the attitude that *nobody* could ever replace Marion, you're going to turn up your nose at applicants who might actually be great. Or, vice versa, if you think, *Well, anyone would do better than the last person*, you may not be as critical as you ought to be.

 Confirmation bias. This is a well-known form of human bias—the idea that we like things that prove us right! Here's how it often plays out in hiring: "Sheryl's resume says she has done marketing work in the past… I bet she'll be *great* at marketing for *our* brand!" And just like that, a perception is set without much evidence to back it up.

So, what's my point? For starters, it's important to take a minute to reflect on your own biases—because you've probably got some; we all do! Also make sure multiple people are involved with recruitment, if possible, and that you can compensate for each other's blind spots.

After you take a good look at what your goals are for the prospective team member, you need to decide if he or she will be a full-time member of your team or an independent contractor.

When to Hire a Contractor

I'm a big believer in teams—and generally speaking, when we talk about workplace teams, we're talking about employees. In some cases, though, the best way to build a team is to augment it with contractors and freelancers. Considering your need and the stage of your company's growth, working with a contractor may make the most sense.

How do you know when it's better to hire a contractor than to hire someone full time? Let me offer a few points for you to ponder. It's best to hire a contractor when:

1. **You have a fluctuating workload and need some flexibility.** It can be costly—and demoralizing—to be in a constant cycle of hiring and firing employees. If you find that your workload is highly variable, or perhaps that it has seasonal spikes, bringing in contractors can help you manage the workload without so much internal pruning.

2. **You need someone highly specialized.** If you're looking for a jack-of-all-trades, you may want to bring someone on full time—but if you need one very specific skillset, a contractor can likely provide it without the need for any training. This can lead to greater productivity.

3. **Your resources are limited.** Simply put, contractors usually cost less than employees, as you won't have to cover things like insurance, office space, etc. That's not to say that employees can't be totally worth it sometimes, of course—but if you have a severely limited staffing budget, a contractor may enable you to get more bang for your buck.

There's no one way to create a team, and even with contractors in the mix you can work toward a common goal. There are many places to find contractors to do almost any kind of work; websites like Fiverr and Upwork are sites where you can hire independent contractors on a project-by-project basis, as well as hourly or full time. If you go with this option, thoroughly check out the site regarding fees, etc., especially if you're on a limited budget.

Chapter 5

HIRING
ON A LIMITED BUDGET

**Don't Let Money Hinder You
From Assembling Your Dream Team!**

Want to know the secret to hiring the *very best* employees in your industry and creating a team *loaded* with all-stars? It's really pretty simple. Call up all the ace talents you know and ask how much you'd have to pay them to come work for you. Whatever number they throw out, make it your new employee's salary. And there you go!

Of course, I'm being silly, but I'm trying to make a point. If money were no object, hiring great talents would probably be very easy.

When you have a limited budget, though—as all businesses do—hiring can be harder. There may be some great talents you'd like to poach, yet you fear that you simply don't have the resources to make it worth their while.

Thankfully, there are ways to work around this. As a speaker and thought leader in the field of team building, I've witnessed some great strategies for hiring top talents, even while on a tight budget. Let me share a few of them with you.

 Know the value of outsourcing. There may be certain tasks that you can simply outsource to someone rather than bringing on a full-time, salaried staff member. This can save you some money on payroll and benefits, which will open more doors for when you *do* hire salaried team members.

 Play up your small size. Believe it or not, many top talents leave bigger companies for smaller ones— even taking pay cuts to do so—in order to enjoy new challenges and autonomy. When recruiting, use your company's size as a selling point—not something to be embarrassed about.

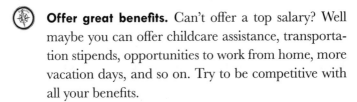

Offer great benefits. Can't offer a top salary? Well maybe you can offer childcare assistance, transportation stipends, opportunities to work from home, more vacation days, and so on. Try to be competitive with all your benefits.

Make use of your existing employees. Spend some time chatting with your engaged, loyal team members about some of *their* connections. Ask them to refer new employees to you and trust them to present your company in the best possible light.

Don't let money hinder you from trying to assemble your dream team! You still have to spend money to make money. Many of your hiring challenges and concerns can be alleviated in the hiring process if you just ask the right questions.

Ask the Right Questions to Hire Great Talents

Job interviews aren't like they used to be. Once upon a time, it was possible for an interviewee to effectively feel "ambushed" by a strange or unexpected interview question. Today, there are countless career sites on the Internet that provide a full rundown of any and all possible interview questions. Plus, in this era of robust focus on company culture, more and more interviewers are asking questions like, "What color crayon are you?" Job applicants practically *expect* to get off-the-wall questions like these.

It's simply very hard to surprise them.

So what does this mean for your recruiting? It means that if you really want to evaluate someone's talent, you need to shy away from easily rehearsed questions and instead ask things that really prove ingenuity and creative, critical thinking. The following are some suggestions for the interview.

1. First, I recommend looking at glassdoor.com and other career sites to see what some of the most common and predictable questions are. You probably know some of them just off the top of your head such as: Where do you see yourself in five years? What are your greatest strengths and weaknesses? The list goes on. Scratch these altogether; there's no sense wasting time with questions that applicants can rehearse the answers to so easily.

2. I recommend avoiding questions that effectively ask the applicant to repeat information from his or her resume. You know where they went to school, where they worked before, and so on. Why waste time asking for a recap of these things?

3. Be careful about historical questions, too. Asking an applicant how he or she dealt with a problem at one company, ten years ago, may have little to do with your company and its unique culture.

4. A better approach is to interview for problem-solving abilities. Ask your job applicant how he or she would identify and solve problems in the first week on the job. Ask for a step-by-step process or some best practices. You can even provide the applicant with the summary of a real problem he or she will face on Day 1 and ask for a potential solution.

5. Ask applicants to do a little forecasting—looking forward to the future of the company or simply the future

of the industry, predicting trends and offering their vision.

As a speaker and author in the leadership arena, I know that recruiting is where great company cultures are built. Once you find the right people, the next step is to make sure they are integrated into your culture to ensure proper onboarding.

Helping New Hires Through Onboarding

Why do new hires fail?

This is one of the fundamental problems that any HR professional or leader must address sooner or later. Every now and then there may be a new employee who turns out to be a poor fit for the company, and that's not necessarily your fault. When a *lot* of new hires end up leaving or being dismissed prematurely, though, it points to an issue more systemic—and significant.

There are several possible answers to why new hires fail. In some cases, it may be a recruiting issue; maybe the employee was truly *never* a good fit, and somehow slipped through the interview and screening processes. Maybe expectations were not communicated on the front end, or maybe feedback was not given to help the employee improve and adapt.

In many cases, though, the problem is an inadequate onboarding process. What is onboarding all about? It really boils down to integrating the new hire into your company culture as quickly and as seamlessly as possible. This means helping the new hire feel comfortable with the position and its responsibilities, with other team members and supervisors, and with company values and policies.

As you consider your onboarding processes, it might be helpful to think about what new hires are looking for. According to one study, new hires are looking for the following in an onboarding process:

- **76 percent** of new hires say that on-the-job training is the most important part.

- **73 percent** say that a review of all company policies and procedures is helpful.

- **59 percent** want a company tour and demonstrations of all the equipment they are expected to use.

- **And a little over half** say that having a buddy or mentor is helpful.

Here's something else from that same study that might surprise you—new hires do not necessarily want HR team members to show them the ropes. Instead, they would rather be trained by their managers and supervisors. That's what makes them feel most comfortable. HR can and should have a role in creating the onboarding process, but it's critical to enlist management and to have them play an active role of their own.

With that said, HR can do much to facilitate a smooth onboarding process. Here's one consideration—it all starts with advance planning. You don't want to overwhelm a new hire with endless rulebooks and forms to fill out on Day 1. That's the kind of thing to e-mail in advance, and to cover as best you can during the recruiting process.

It is also helpful to set the tone for what your company culture is like. Express to potential new hires what your company values and mission are—even during the interview. You can discuss the details on the first day, but during the interview, it's good to give a broad picture.

Remember how critical the onboarding process is—and how daunting it can be! As a leader, it's important to work with your HR professional, your roles should be to help the new hire through it, and to position them for success within your organization.

Effective Employee Retention Strategy

Now that you've hired your team and they are acclimated to your culture, how do you retain them? This is a common struggle in every business so let's look at the *four hurdles you need to overcome to improve employee retention.*

Leaders, employers, and HR representatives pour countless hours into each employee—grooming them, training them, investing in them, making them into integral members of the team. But sometimes, just when you turn a good employee into a superstar, that employee jumps ship, heads to a different company, and leaves you back at the dock.

If that's not the most frustrating part of team leadership, it's got to be high on the list. Of course you probably do what you can to enhance employee retention, but sometimes that's easier said than accomplished, and the hurdles to proper retention are numerous.

It starts with hiring. The *first big hurdle* to employee retention is bringing on board the wrong employees in the first place. Team-building starts with the hiring process—and if you're recruiting employees who are a bad fit, don't be surprised when they don't stick around for the long haul.

Are you experiencing a lot of employee turnover? That may mean you need to go back and reflect on your hiring standards. Make sure you have clearly defined job descriptions and a clearly articulated company culture, and that you hire with both of these in mind.

Another hurdle to retention—employees who get hired then quickly realize they have no clear way to advance in the company—and no clear future with your organization.

Employees want to know you're investing in their career development; showing them that, though, can seem tricky.

What's an employer to do in this case? Two things, actually. One, check in with employees regularly to talk about their career goals and be open with them about possible avenues for advancing in the company. And two, make sure to invest in team training—a great way to show employees you care about their development.

The *third hurdle* to retention is lack of proper communication. Employees like to know that they have an open dialogue with the boss, or at the very least with the HR manager. It's important that you keep those channels of dialogue open.

Having an open-door policy is helpful, but one formal step you can take is to implement an annual review process and really take it seriously—a great way of showing employees that you have an ongoing interest in them.

Often the *biggest hurdle* to retention is *money and benefits*. Although you want to provide your employees with enticing benefits and competitive salaries, sometimes the budget just doesn't allow for it. That's when you have to get creative by offering cost-effective employee benefits like flexible scheduling, work-from-home options, professional development events, and the like.

I want to emphasize the importance of ongoing training to develop your team and build a stronger culture. The companies that place an emphasis on continuing education have employees who are more productive, are loyal to the company, and refer their friends when opportunities arise for positions in the organization.

It is important to consider these four hurdles and how each plays a major role in retaining employees and preventing them from seeking other opportunities.

Why Employees Leave in Waves—and How to Stop Them

On the one hand, the equation is simple about why employees leave in waves—they like to work at a company where they feel important and valued. They want to be able to use their talents and their time effectively, to really make an impact; and they want to know that their efforts are noticed and appreciated.

On the other hand...well, maybe it's not so simple at all! Valuing employees is about more than just salary and benefits. It also means providing an environment that fosters good, productive work. It means facilitating mutual respect and a true team dynamic. It means offering clear trajectories for professional development and career advancement—and oh yeah...you need to do all of this on a pretty tight HR budget.

Why Good Employees Quit

So where do you possibly begin? How do you start the process of showing employees that they matter to you, and how do you keep the best ones from jumping ship *en masse?*

Start with this realization—*employees don't quit the job, they quit the boss*. And if you have a lot of turnover, a lot of employees leaving in waves, you can rest assured that the problem isn't them—it's the boss, you. If not you, it is their immediate supervisor.

With that word of tough love out of the way, the following are some very good reasons why your good employees quit—and some suggestions for keeping them on board.

1. **The best people are burdened with too many responsibilities.** I recently met an accountant who was obviously supremely gifted, exceptionally good at her job; as a corporate bookkeeper, she was invaluable. When the company's HR manager quit, this amazing accountant was given HR responsibilities, even though she didn't want them, didn't have any background in that field, and frankly didn't have time for the additional workload. She was unable to devote herself to accounting excellence, and she became deeply unhappy in her work. Do you see the problem? When you have an excellent employee, make sure you give that employee the freedom to do what he or she does best, rather than burdening with additional duties.

2. **Micromanaging.** Many executives and managers are perfectionists by nature. That's great. But maybe the skill you need to work on is trusting people. In theory, you hired your employees for a reason—you saw something in them. So let them do their work without peering over their shoulder, or else you risk seeing them go somewhere their talents will be better appreciated.

3. **No support.** Not supporting your employees is almost the opposite of micromanaging. Your employees don't

want to be micromanaged, but they do want to know you're available to answer questions or provide direction as needed. Never in the office? Well, don't be surprised if your employees quit to find a company where they think there is a more personal and devoted support system.

4. **Clueless about team dynamics.** Two quick questions: What are the biggest sources of conflict on your team? Who are the employees most and least likely to collaborate together? If you don't know the answers, you're probably not really building a good team or using individual talents to their full potential. Don't think your employees won't notice that.

5. **Inefficient and unproductive meetings.** People don't like having their time wasted.

6. **Lack of communication.** Your employees want to know they have a role in something bigger—they need to know the company's vision and mission. But if you're oriented on tasks and not the big picture, your employees will feel like pawns in your personal secret game.

These are just some of the behaviors that can cause great employees to grow frustrated, and leave your company in waves—so if you want to prevent that from happening, prevent these *behaviors* from becoming *habits*.

It all comes down to self-awareness, which leads back to the first chapter: "Success Begins with You." So, are you the problem or the solution? Self-analysis is essential, especially when employees are leaving in waves.

My personal experience is based on the fact that I thought the problem was everybody else until I recognized the pattern and had to come to the realization that I was the problem. I was a terrible boss…who became determined to improve as a leader immediately!

Boost Your Employee Retention— Without Breaking the Bank

People will leave even if you pay them more money—especially if they simply don't like working with you or for the company.

However, if they do like working with you and the company but have expressed some displeasure, you could offer them all big, regular raises—but if you're like most of the business owners and HR managers I've met, you probably don't have the resources necessary to make that offer a viable option.

So, what do you do instead? Some cost-effective options were mentioned previously to keep your employees on the team for years to come. Let's look at these ways more closely.

Start by reminding yourself that employees don't quit their jobs—they quit their bosses. But of course, you don't want to let it get to that point. You want to prevent the mass exodus by investing in employee retention—as affordably as you can. And to that end, I have a few ideas for you to consider.

The following are some affordable ways to invest in employee retention that you can implement immediately:

 Provide training. I say this all the time because I really believe in it. Offering training shows your employees that you care about their development as people and employees; it shows that you are investing in them over the long haul. It sends a powerful message, and it's a message that most employees really appreciate. So, invest in some on-site training options at your company; it doesn't need to be every week, but do offer it routinely. Computer training, marketing seminars, mentorship programs, trips to outside seminars and workshops—there are plenty of ways to make this happen.

Soup up your benefits. You may not be able to afford giving everyone more vacation time, but perhaps you can allow them to use their benefits more flexibly— providing flexible work hours, sabbaticals, or a Paid Time Off policy that gives employees more control over how they use their (sick, vacation, personal) days.

Offer metrics. Your employees want to see that their hard work is actually accomplishing something. They want to see results—so show them. Provide your employees with data and reports that indicate how their efforts are paying off. Encourage them to keep up the good work.

Be the best. Hone in on your company's competitive advantage, and then encapsulate that in your company mission and values statements. Make sure your employees know they're working for a company that's special, that they are playing for the winning team!

Open your door. Employees are more likely to stay with a company where they feel supported— so whether you're the CEO, HR manager, group leader, or immediate supervisor, make sure you're approachable. You'll be surprised how far this open-door policy can go!

The best leaders understand this because they follow the advice in Chapter 6: "Communicate to Activate!"

Chapter 6

COMMUNICATE TO
ACTIVATE!

To Build a Better Culture,
The Key Is *Communication*.

Communication impacts everything—how well your team members work together, how much they accomplish, how engaged they are, and on down the list. Most accurately, communication shapes your culture—so whether you're looking to overhaul your company culture or simply improve what you already have in place, it's never a bad time to review your workplace communication practices.

The following are a few recommendations for more effective communication.

Set the Standards

First things first—there should never be any question at your company about what is and isn't appropriate workplace communication.

Joking around, informality, casual banter—if conversations cross a line, there will be consequences. But, the line has to be clearly set and cited in the employee handbook so everyone knows what is acceptable and what is not. There should be no murky, gray area about what's accepted in terms of workplace communication.

Clarify the Terminology

Do you prefer the term *clients* or *customers?* How about *guests?* And are your team members *employees*—or would you rather them think of themselves as *associates?*

Once again, the employee handbook is an ideal place to clearly spell out your preferred terms in shaping your workplace communication.

Focus on Clarity

Defined terminology is one thing, but jargon is quite another. In fact, overly technical language can impede clarity and confuse people, which is the enemy of clear workplace communication.

Keep your company culture as free of jargon as possible. Review your own communication habits for any vague buzzwords and remove them from your internal communications.

Use Technology Intentionally

Want to adopt Skype, Slack, Zoom.US, WhatsApp, or some other instant messaging program within your office?

By all means, do so—just be clear about why you're doing it, and how those tools are meant to be used. Make sure *technology has a clearly defined role* within your company culture.

Go Beyond Words

Remember that communication isn't just about the words you write or speak. Body language and tone of voice can also convey deep meaning. Be mindful of this and think about ways in which you might need to modify your own approach to communication.

As the leader, you set the tone for communication. I like to say communication is not what a person says, it's how the other person hears what was said.

We all hear things differently based on our past experiences and references. Because I work internationally as an executive coach and speaker, I make sure to use the terminology of the country that I'm working in as best as I can.

That means really doing your homework so that you can communicate effectively in any circumstance. This is very important, especially when it comes to feedback with your employees and clients.

Is Your Feedback Truly Constructive?

When you're a solutions-oriented leader, you can't be afraid of confrontation. Part of *your* job is making sure that everyone else is doing *their* job correctly—and if there's an issue on your team, it's up to you to address it.

There's a right way and a wrong way to do that, however; and when it comes time to offer feedback, it's important to be thoughtful in your approach. The purpose of feedback is to be constructive—to provide scaffolding on which your team members can build better skills and higher achievements. When offered carelessly, feedback can simply come across as critical, mean, or rude—all of which can squash confidence and creativity and lower your team's morale.

The question is, how can leaders ensure that the feedback they offer is genuinely productive, not just critical? Here are a few strategies to keep in mind:

 Constructive feedback is specific. Telling someone, "That's bad" isn't helpful, and in fact it's not even feedback; it's just nastiness. Real feedback focuses on something specific and offers a benchmark that is both measurable and achievable. Give your team members a target to aim for and a timeline to achieve it.

 Constructive feedback is private. Your aim should never be to punish or to embarrass, even if a team member has made a big error. A good rule of thumb is to always praise publicly and critique privately. You may consider following up on your private meetings with something written—a quick e-mail reminder of the feedback you offered and the goals you laid out for the team member. The point here is simply to ensure that the employee doesn't forget, which is an easy thing to do!

Constructive feedback is not personal. Saying that a presentation is poorly organized is fine; saying that the person is disorganized is not. Constructive feedback focuses on a concrete situation, not on the traits of the individual.

Constructive feedback is continuous. Don't offer a critique and then forget it; make sure to follow up, and that the team member knows his or her efforts are not being overlooked. Feedback is a process, and the more you invest in it, the more likely it is to yield the desired effect.

Great leaders are unafraid to offer feedback, and in fact they know that feedback is a true gift—so long as it's offered in the right spirit, with the right specificity, and with the right level of follow-through.

As mentioned in a previous chapter, I like to use a technique called *Like Best, Next Time,* which is excellent for giving constructive feedback. I know that we are toughest on ourselves when we make a mistake. The last thing people want is to be told about the mistake they just made. However, if we can communicate the message in a way that's not offensive and the employee can self-analyze, we can expect a longtime correction of a potential bad habit.

For example, let's say Sally sent an e-mail to a client without formal approval because she likes to be efficient. Here is how the conversation might go:

Dr. Rick: "Sally, do you know what I *Like Best* about you? You're efficient, positive, and a great team player. *Next Time* could you run that letter by me for approval so I can make sure the numbers accurately reflect what we can deliver?"

Dr. Rick: "Sally, what did you *Like Best* and what do you think is the best way for us to approach this *Next Time?*"

When Sally figures out what the best approach is, she will own it! I have been using Like Best and Next Time since my third year in business. I only started to use it after I was ready to receive constructive feedback about my skills, or lack thereof, as a leader from my mentor.

Do You Accept Constructive Feedback?

I've said in the past that one of the greatest gifts a leader can give to team members is the gift of honest *feedback*. Taking the time to provide a quick word of encouragement or constructive criticism can go a long way toward showing employees that they are noticed and valued; that you are invested in their future and their place on the team.

There is a flipside to that great gift, as well. A hallmark of leadership is that you don't just offer feedback, but also welcome it in your own professional life. Great leaders actively court feedback from colleagues and from employees—and don't get their feathers ruffled when the feedback is less than positive.

It's a simple fact of life that no one likes having our shortcomings pointed out to us, yet other people can often identify our faults more accurately than we can.

When you're willing to graciously accept that kind of feedback—not bristling or getting defensive, but actually engaging with it and implementing changes—it shows that you're a humble leader. It shows that what you care about is seeing *all* members of your team improve their performance and get better results over time.

When your team members come to you with feedback, it's important to accept and even embrace it—not brush it aside. Some tips for taking constructive feedback *well* include:

- **Don't take it personally.** Remember that everyone has blind spots and skills that need further developing. The fact that you have some areas to work on does not mean you're a bad person, and that's surely not what your team members want you to think. The goal is for you to get better, and your team members are just trying to help you—not insult you!

- **Specificity is always a good thing.** "You're not a good communicator" is not great feedback; if your team members approach you with something like that, ask them for something more specific. That shows that you really want to improve, and it gives you measurable goals to work toward.

- **Don't be afraid to ask for help!** If your team members identify problem areas, maybe they can also help you brainstorm solutions.

- **Be grateful.** Say thank you for the feedback—remembering that, for your employees, it's probably really hard to approach their boss or manager with words of constructive criticism.

 Offer to return the favor and do an employee appraisal for anyone who comes to you with feedback—not in a tit-for-tat manner, but in the interest of making everyone on the team even better! Remember, feedback is a gift. Give it as well as open yourself to receive it!

One of the first things my mentor shared with me when I was ready to accept feedback and act on it was the four mistakes I had to be aware of and correct immediately when connecting with others.

Four Mistakes When Connecting with People

You know how to communicate—but do you know how to *connect?* And you know how to speak—but are you sure you're *listening*, and giving others a reason to listen to *you?*

These might seem like rudimentary skills, but in our age of social media and smartphones, they're practically endangered!

We *communicate* all the time, and many of us mistake that for connecting. In truth, connecting with people requires a specific set of skills—competencies that you have to work on and nurture all the time.

Learning how to connect with people requires that you first let go of all the small mistakes *preventing* you from *making better connections*. The following are four of the *biggest mistakes* people make when trying to connect with others:

1. **Trying to connect when you don't have the time for it.** If you're in the middle of a thousand other things at work and you simply can't give your full attention to

another human, well, don't. There is nothing wrong with asking to reconvene in five or ten minutes or the next day, after you have your other affairs under control. This is far better than trying to connect when you simply don't have the brain capacity for it!

2. **Not actually listening.** Listening to someone requires more than just hearing the words they speak. It means taking the time to stop and think about what they mean. What are their underlying emotions? What are the *needs* they're bringing to the conversation? Key in to facial expressions, tone of voice, and body language as well as word choice. Focus on *understanding* at a deeper level.

3. **Ignoring your gut.** In the minds of many business professionals, brains are everything; instincts are nothing. In reality, though, you should listen to your gut feelings, which may clue you into issues or complexities that your mind can't yet wrap itself around. If something about a connection feels off to you, there's probably something to that, and you may want to stop and reassess.

4. **Not giving yourself space.** One way to connect better with people is to connect better with yourself—giving yourself a little bit of quiet "me time" each and every day. It may be as simple as a few moments of meditation and self-affirmation at the start of each day, or maybe time during a workout—but make sure you don't force yourself to connect with people all day, every day.

Connecting with people is essential for, well, almost everything—for leadership, sales, and team building, to name just three. These are skills worth working on and will help you as you strive to maintain a robust and engaged company culture.

These were the four areas that were my initial focus in addressing my own weaknesses, and I found that I wasn't alone. Do any of these four mistakes sound familiar to you? If so, let's examine some ways to improve communications with our employees.

How to Improve Communication with Your Employees

What's the single most important factor in the success of a workplace team? Many would say that it's communication. Certainly, as a solutions-oriented leader, you need to be communicating with your employees effectively. Transparent communication ensures that your employees know what is expected of them, and how they can prove successful within your organization; that they feel respected and valued, and that they value *you* as a leader and perhaps even a mentor.

But how can leaders boost their own communication efforts? The following are some action steps I took that dramatically improved my communication with my team.

 Create an environment where communication is open and mutual. Have an open-door policy—perhaps *literally* opening your office door, at least during certain parts of the day—and make it clear that you value your employees' feedback. Don't punish your employees for bringing you their concerns or their constructive criticism.

 Don't mistake *information* for *communication*. Throwing a ton of information at your employees is not the same thing as communicating with them, and in fact it can lead to stress. Don't just offer information, but also the necessary processes for using that information. And when you do dispense information, prioritize.

⊛ **Be generous in your affirmation.** One of the most effective ways to communicate with your employees is to praise them for their achievements and their hard work—which will cultivate better relationships and build better morale.

⊛ **Try to scale back industry lingo and slang.** Of course, you sometimes have to use terminology native to your industry, but remember that this can be daunting or even confusing for newer employees.

⊛ **Always take time to answer questions from your employees.** Your employees need to feel comfortable asking questions—and if you rush through your answers, they won't.

⊛ **Be thoughtful in your written communications.** It's tempting to toss off hastily composed e-mails to your team, but take an extra few minutes to make sure you're conveying the right tone and also providing all pertinent information—dates, times, goals, basic expectations. No plan is a plan to fail.

Remember, communication is a key to morale, to team cohesion, to the achievement of goals—and ultimately, to success. There are also times when a leader must do something that is personally uncomfortable. I'm talking about when a leader has to share bad news. There are several ways you can do this effectively with positive results.

How Great Leaders Share Bad News

Nobody likes to be the bearer of bad news—and when you're a leader, delivering grim tidings can be especially difficult. After all, bad news about the state of the company—or about an error you've made—can have a direct impact on the morale of your employees, on the solidity of the company, and even on their employment status.

So, whether you're fessing up to a big fumble or letting someone know of a pending layoff, it's worth knowing how to deliver bad news *well*. The following are tips to consider:

 Don't lead with an apology. "I'm sorry, but..." is never a good way to start bad news. It may seem like it will make you appear empathetic, but actually it makes you look weak and uncaring—like you could or should be doing something to prevent this bad thing from happening, but all you can muster is a rote apology. Skip the apology—or at least, save it until a more appropriate time—and get straight to the news itself.

Don't be cursory or flippant. Another bad way to begin bad news? "Well, since I have you here..." If you're sharing news that can impact people's lives and livelihoods, you don't want to come across like it's incidental. Plan a time to sit down and talk; give some heads-up that you have news to share.

Don't beat around the bush. It's always best to get right to the point. Overloading your audience with background information or unnecessary lead-up makes it seem like you're nervous about sharing the news itself—and that puts people on edge. More to the point, it undermines your authority.

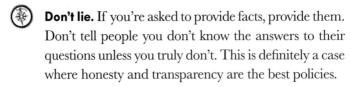 **Don't lie.** If you're asked to provide facts, provide them. Don't tell people you don't know the answers to their questions unless you truly don't. This is definitely a case where honesty and transparency are the best policies.

Don't be ill-prepared. Finally, make sure you spend some time thinking about what you're going to say before you say it; trying to riff or improvise your way through bad news is the surest way to stumble into some of these other issues I've brought up.

Leadership is critical during difficult days or challenging seasons. When you have bad news to deliver, make sure you rise to the occasion.

I watched an amazing movie titled *The Darkest Hour*, with Gary Oldman as Winston Churchill. Many times, Churchill had to deliver bad news to the British people; however, the delivery of his message, including the tonality and style, is ultimately what swayed Parliament, the British people, and the King of England to get behind him to fight back and win the war against the Nazis.

The leader who is prepared will set the tone and the direction that the news will take them. Remember, "Teams go where you go!"

Ralph Ledee is also a solutions-oriented leader. He is the managing partner of International Liquors Tobacco and Trading (ILTT) on St. Maarten—and he understands about delivering bad news.

On September 5, 1995, Ralph survived Hurricane Lewis that pounded St. Maarten for 36 hours and destroyed his house and business. It took three-plus years for Ralph to rebuild the business.

On September 6, 2017, when Hurricane Irma and its 250 mph winds hit, making it the strongest storm ever in the Atlantic to make landfall, it destroyed Ralph's house and business again! This was not the first time he had to make tough decisions and deliver bad news to his employees.

Pledges of $450 million in aid were made; however, only $50 million was received, making the road to recovery even more difficult. The writing was on the wall and Ralph could see it clearly. In order to survive, he focused on solutions and made a plan. Ralph knew he had get a grip on things quickly and make tough decisions to maintain the business and start the rebuilding process.

Ralph broke his plan down to four phases:

1. Survival

2. Rebuilding

3. Operating

4. Excelling

He told me the storm brought people together, but he had to be honest with his employees about how long the survival and rebuilding would take. His honesty actually gave many of his employees the opportunity to make a decision and plan a fresh start for themselves and their families.

Sometimes delivering the bad news includes sharing the big picture and the hard facts of the journey ahead.

Expressing Workplace Gratitude

Another way a leader can turn bad into good is by expressing gratitude. I've written about thankfulness before, and in fact the concept of gratitude figures prominently in my first book. Expressing your appreciation for team members is a powerful way to foster an open, collaborative, and tight-knit team dynamic; it's also a key ingredient in employee retention.

Yet, knowing *how* to express gratitude in the workplace can seem elusive. Not to worry. I offer six suggestions for cultivating *thankfulness* in your office.

1. **Don't wait.** First and foremost, make thankfulness part of your daily work routine. Don't wait until Thanksgiving. Don't wait until the end of the year. Don't wait until you're leading a project or directing other employees. Start saying thank you today to anyone who helps make your professional life more fruitful. Get in the habit of expressing gratitude often.

2. **Remember that nobody accomplishes anything alone.** You're part of a team. Your success is, at least, somewhat contingent on your team members; likewise, the role you play in the workplace has an impact on everyone else's success. Remember that you're part of something bigger and adopt a humble attitude about workplace achievements.

3. **Provide opportunities for your team members to express their gratitude.** While you don't necessarily want to force gratitude, you should provide outlets for people to say thanks—maybe through bulletin boards

or gratitude walls or through holiday gift exchanges. Some employees may wish to express their thanks but are unsure of appropriate ways to do so. Give them the avenue they need!

4. **Be intentional in thanking your employees.** On a more formal level, you can create an employee-of-the-month program, blog spotlights, or other forums for showing employees you care. Make sure to highlight the work of chronically under-thanked team members, too—the people whose work isn't necessarily flashy but is nevertheless essential for the success of your team.

5. **Be thankful during tough times.** Make sure you say thanks to your team, not just during seasons of plenty, but also during seasons of hardship—and in the wake of crises, in particular. Learning to say thank you isn't just a seasonal thing; for true leaders, it's a skillset to cultivate year-round.

6. **Bonus Tip:** Years ago, people would write thank-you notes and letters to clients and associates and that art has been lost for the most part. If you want to stand out from the crowd as a leader and professional, write thank-you notes to the people you work with, family members, and anyone you can think of!

If you write five notes a day Monday through Friday for thirty days (a few sentences will do, you don't have to write a novel), you only need two minutes per thank-you note for total of ten minutes per day. Watch the appreciation and your business grow. I guarantee it!

Communications Training

Sometimes when we analyze ourselves and our team, we recognize that in order to grow and truly become successful we may have to look for additional training outside the workplace in order to communicate more effectively.

Is the ability to communicate clearly something you're born with, or something you learn? It's probably a little bit of both. Some people are just naturally better communicators than others. At the same time, communication skills can be honed, fostered, and refined. There is much to be said for communication training as a method for developing your prowess for effectively and constructively conveying your point—and making connections with others.

Many of the companies I work with ask me to conduct training on presentation skills and communication. Communications training can benefit individuals, but it can also benefit teams. In fact, it might be advantageous for you to invest in communications training for *your* team.

I'll let you in on a secret—all teams can benefit from communications training on some level. An investment in communications training is never going to be anything but a boon for your company culture.

With that said, there are some specific, telltale signs that your team may need to collectively brush up on its communication skills:

 You have tried to explain the company's priorities to your team members—yet they all seem to have their own entirely *different* lists of priorities.

 Your team members are prone to interrupt one another—or worse, to interrupt customers—trying to get their point made rather than seeking true understanding.

- The same arguments and conflicts continue to arise in your workplace, over and over again.

- Some or all team members use disparaging or belittling language to speak about one another.

- You receive a high number of customer service complaints.

- Project after project misses the deadline or is hastily completed at the eleventh hour.

- You or your team members hoard or withhold information—using it as leverage rather than freely sharing it for the group's benefit.

- Meaningful communication is missing at your workplace; your team members don't collaborate, don't answer e-mails, remain silent during huddles, or they fail to offer any feedback.

Any of these points reveal a potential communications breakdown in your workplace—but nothing you can't remedy with on-site training. That's an investment your entire team will benefit from—and one you won't forget.

I have found that bringing a third-party coach or trainer from outside your industry gives you a different perspective on your business. An outside consultant or executive coach wants to see everyone win and keeps the team focused on the finish line and away from the blame game.

If your communication with your team, your clients, and your family is not effective, you have a major challenge—and it's time for Engagement in the Workplace!

Chapter 7

ENGAGEMENT IN THE
WORKPLACE

**Building Engagement Has a Real,
Bottom-line Impact.**

Employee engagement remains a lively topic among today's leaders, coaches, and Human Resources professionals—a topic that invites plenty of nuanced discussion, but also demands a big-picture view.

Let's start with some simple facts and figures. About what percentage of the workforce would you say is truly engaged? According to a recent Gallup survey, the picture is pretty grim. An article in *Forbes* magazine summarizes: "According to Gallup's State of the Global Workplace report, only 15 percent of employees worldwide are engaged in their jobs—meaning that they are emotionally invested in committing their time, talent, and energy in adding value to their team and advancing the organization's initiatives."[1]

And that's not all. "More Gallup research shows that employee disengagement costs the United States upwards of $550 billion a year in lost productivity," the article in *Forbes* continues.[2]

These are obviously not very good numbers. Employees represent a company's most precious assets—and if your employees aren't engaged, it means you're neither taking care of them properly nor getting as much out of them as you *could*, plain and simple.

It might help to consider employee engagement across a few different categories. First, if Gallup is to be believed, there are engaged employees—roughly 15 percent of the workforce. These are the team members who are emotionally committed. They excel at what they do, and their talents are leveraged fully.

Then there are those who are simply not engaged; Gallup estimates that about 67 percent of the workforce fits into this category. These are the employees who do the bare minimum. They don't cause problems, per se, but neither do they have any sense of mission or of goals.

"They are less likely to be customer-focused and are not concerned about productivity or company profitability," according to the article in *Forbes*. "These team members are both a threat and great opportunity—because with the proper approach, they can be transformed into engaged employees that thrive in the organization."[3]

Finally, representing about 18 percent of the workforce, there are those employees who are actively disengaged—those who have basically checked out. They are negative, they are toxic, and they are probably not redeemable; frankly, you're better off removing them from your team as soon as you can.

It's worth considering your own team in this light. How would you categorize each employee? Are there employees who are not engaged, but could be brought around? Are there employees who should simply be terminated? Or are you already doing a great job keeping your team inspired, motivated, and emotionally invested?

Take some time to think about the answers to these questions, which will provide you with some direction for your future efforts at employee engagement. As you see, it has an enormous effect on your bottom line.

Employee Engagement and Your Bottom Line

Employers have learned, slowly but surely, that when your team members have an *emotional investment* in the company, they're going to do better work. So, working to build engagement isn't just about keeping peace or making your people happy; it has a real, bottom-line impact.

Don't believe me? Let me list just a few concrete ways in which you can actually *measure* the results of employee engagement and how it can affect you.

Employee engagement plays a definite role and has a major impact in a number of areas; the following are six areas that are most crucial to your company.

1. **Productivity.** An invested and engaged workforce will outperform a workforce that's lackadaisical or unmotivated—all the time. Study after study confirms that when you engage your employees, you get more high-quality work out of them, not less.

2. **Retention.** Employees who are engaged in their jobs are less likely to leave for greener pastures. Makes sense, right? And that, in turn, saves you the cost of recruiting and onboarding new people.

3. **Morale.** Workplace happiness isn't just some pie-in-the-sky ideal. High morale has been linked to both productivity and retention—just what I've been saying. While employees who are unhappy are more likely to do sloppy work and to look for new opportunities elsewhere.

4. **Innovation.** Engagement can manifest as creativity. Think of some of the great tech breakthroughs of the last decade. How many of them do you think were engineered by people who were bored and unengaged?

5. **Communication.** Employees who are engaged are more likely to communicate clearly and proactively with their colleagues. Again, it just makes sense, right?

6. **Recruitment.** Employees who are engaged in what they do and who feel happy at work are more likely to recommend the company to others—and that can really help with recruitment. Employee engagement is crucial to your professional success. You can really track its results—and that makes it something worth investing in.

Review these six areas you just read and calculate the Return On Investment (ROI) for improving each one. I think the truth will be obvious. Employee engagement must become a top priority if you want your team to become the best possible.

What Does Workplace Engagement Really Look Like?

As a keynote speaker, one of the topics I love to discuss most is *employee engagement*. What I've noticed is that many organizations are really *hungry* to discuss this topic, yet there's often a misperception about what employee engagement actually *is*.

Think about it for a second. Do you know how to define the term? If someone asked you what employee engagement is, how would you respond?

It's one of those buzzwords that we accept without really unpacking it—so let me try to clear up some things. First, a few words about what employee engagement is *not*. For one thing, engagement is not happiness—not exactly. Sure, engagement may make many of your employees happier at the office—but if happiness was all there was to it, you could just buy a keg and a ping-pong table for your break room and be done with it.

Happiness is not the same thing as engagement—and neither is satisfaction. You may have plenty of satisfied employees who are perfectly willing to do their job from 9 to 5 each day, but they won't necessarily go the extra mile or even feel particularly loyal to the organization.

So what *is* employee engagement? Here's my simple definition—*engagement is the measure of how emotionally **committed** your employees are to the team.*

To put it another way, *your employees are **engaged** when they show up for more than a paycheck.* They're engaged when they feel like their work is meaningful, and that the organization is doing something significant.

As such, engagement doesn't necessarily look like employee parties, socialization, or games—though those things can help. Employee engagement is founded on something more basic—ensuring that employees believe they are part of the organization and that you have invested in them as integral members of your team.

Some of the most fundamental hallmarks of employee engagement include: soliciting employee feedback; genuinely listening to them; ensuring they are clear on the vision of the organization; and showing that you want them around for the long haul—something you can do by providing opportunities for professional training and development.

I call it being REAL! People are people, and when you show your team that you care, that you really have their best interest in mind, you will truly be engaging your team.

Why Growth Is the Key to Employee Engagement

Study after study confirms that when it comes to employee engagement, one of *the* critical factors is *development*. Employees need to know that they have opportunities to grow, to broaden their horizons, to deepen their skillsets.

To keep your employees engaged, offering these *growth opportunities* is absolutely essential—and here's why.

When there's no room for growth, employees feel stagnant.

There is a real historic record for this statement. In 2010, surveys found that employee perception of company-sponsored growth opportunities was at an all-time low, across the board. And that makes sense, given the high unemployment rate and the fact that many company training programs were being done away with. Opportunities for promotion, meanwhile, were dwindling.

As a result, employee engagement numbers also plummeted. Employees across the United States felt like they didn't really have any way to move onward and upward—and their passion for work dropped because of it.

Growth opportunities help everyone.

By contrast, recent years have seen more and more companies offering their employees chances to grow—educational opportunities as well as wider on-the-job experience. It's not surprising that this motivates employees, especially younger ones who value career development more than any other workplace benefits—including salary!

But growth opportunities aren't only good for the employees. They're also key for the company. They enhance the employer brand by revealing that you really care about supporting your people in the long term. When it comes to recruiting top talents, this is exceedingly beneficial.

You can make an investment in your team members.

Ultimately, growth opportunities—whether training or promotions, or simply more delegated responsibilities—show that you believe in the employees and have confidence in their ability to thrive. Make your employees see that *they* are your most important assets.

Emotion and Engagement

The best way I know to engage people is through emotion. Everyone wants love, appreciation, and respect. If you give it, you will get it!

Do your employees show up to work each day engaged with your mission and ready to do their best work to advance the company's goals? Or are they just there for a paycheck? Worse yet, are they just doing time?

Far too often, team members fall into the latter camp—and of course that means they're not *engaged*. Boosting employee engagement is a main focus for many team leaders, and there are a lot of schools of thought about how best to go about it.

Right now, I want to propose something simple to engage your employees in a meaningful way—think in terms of *emotions*. As an employer, ask yourself, *What are the **emotional drivers** for employee engagement?*

What am I talking about? Simply that employee engagement is often rooted in feelings—feelings of being appreciated, of being wanted, of doing something meaningful, and of being part of something bigger than their immediate circumstances. This is one of the cornerstones of transformational leadership.

Let me show you what I mean. The following is a quick guide to emotional thinking as it relates to employee engagement:

Your employees want to feel proud. One of the strongest emotional drivers is a sense of pride; your employees want to feel like they are doing good, high-quality work that *matters*. They want to feel like they can go home and brag about the good things they accomplished during their work day. Does your organization promote this sense of pride? Are you giving your people meaningful work to do and clearly showing the difference it makes?

Your employees want to feel recognized. Your employees want their good work to be noticed, and their efforts to be appreciated. Do you make a point of praising good work? Of saying thank you to your employees? Of passing along positive feedback from clients and customers?

Your employees want to feel like they are growing and improving. Your team members also want to feel like they have opportunities for professional development—that the time spent at your company is sharpening them, not making them go stagnant. What kinds of professional development opportunities are you offering to your employees?

Your employees want to feel heard. A final emotional driver for employee engagement—your team members want to have voices of their own. Do you welcome their feedback? Do you involve them in decision-making? Do they feel like what they say is heard and taken seriously?

Master Emotional Thinking

When you think in terms of how your employees *feel*—and how they *want* to feel—you can start to think more specifically about employee engagement. This was something that frankly I failed at early in my career. I was focused on Numero Uno, me! When we become other-person focused, the results and the positive feedback are truly outstanding. Remember, it's better to give than to get, and it all starts with you choosing to focus on others!

Employee Engagement Starts with Your Leadership

Employee engagement doesn't actually start with your employees. It starts with *you*, the leader—with the example you set, the culture you build, the commitment you make to inspire your team members.

As an executive coach, I talk with leaders all the time about the efforts they can make—practical, real-world steps—to boost engagement. The following are a few of the practices I most highly recommend.

How Leaders Can Boost Engagement

 Align the Workforce: The members of your team need to be working toward the same thing, headed in the same direction—but how can they do this if they don't have any sense of where the company is headed, or what you're all trying to achieve? As the leader, it falls to you to articulate a clear sense of mission—and to make plain how every project, every task, and every employee contributes to that mission.

Empower Your Managers: Those who are in direct managerial roles—interacting with employees daily—are the ones you need to invest in first. Develop their skills of engagement and empowerment. Provide them with direction in how they can listen, set clear expectations, and deliver feedback that is truly constructive. Make sure the managers are all on the same page about employee engagement.

Emphasize Fairness: You can't afford to have employees disenfranchised because they think you're playing favorites. In everything you do—from resource allocation to how you make sales—make sure you're applying principles of fairness.

Create Leaders: Don't settle for employees who do a workmanlike job every day. Invest in promising talents and encourage them in leadership development. Help them develop the skills of engaging and motivating other employees and provide opportunities for them to prove themselves.

Measure! As the solutions-oriented leader of your team, one of your most important responsibilities is measuring results—and that includes the results of engagement efforts. Use surveys and other employee feedback programs to benchmark your progress.

These are some pragmatic steps leaders can take as they look to do their part in enhancing employee engagement.

Which brings me to the importance of engaging the new employees on your team and how it benefits the company culture.

How to Engage New Employees on Your Team

It's tough being the newbie. That's true when you're in grade school and it's still true when you're a grown-up: Coming into a new workplace environment—especially one with a tight-knit team dynamic—can be challenging, and more than a little daunting.

It's not just hard for the new employee, though. Leaders and managers can sometimes face an uphill climb in grafting the new employee into the existing team culture. That's not the employee's fault. It's just hard to step into a program that's already been established; it's hard to find your place when everyone else has already settled into their role.

So how do you help your new employees fit in? It takes a concentrated effort. Here are a few ways you can get on the right track from the start:

 Engage the new employee early on, scheduling group activities or collaborative projects even on Day 1. Also—and I say this all the time, but it's important— make collaboration implicit to all project assignments. For example, tell New Hire Bill that his job is to work with Claire and Dan on Project X and tell Claire and Dan that *their* job is to work in tandem with Bill.

 Schedule lunches, coffee breaks, or quick face-to-face meetings with more senior team members. Make these regular, especially at the beginning. Give the new hire a chance to get to know you, to ask questions as needed, and to offer feedback. Use these meetings to assess the engagement process.

In keeping with that last point, make sure you view onboarding as a two-way street. Always provide your new hire with a chance to express his or her opinions, and to let you know how things are going.

Be explicit in communicating your values. What's your company's mission? What is its vision? How would you characterize its culture? You can't just expect new hires to *know* these things; you must make them plain. This should be the centerpiece of the onboarding process.

Invest in training! New hires like to be trained because it gives them confidence to do their job better, and it proves that you have an investment in them. Note that training does not always have to be formal, and in fact more *informal* opportunities to participate and observe in group projects can be most helpful. When I work with a company as an executive coach, I make it a point of personally meeting the new employees and placing them on a program to improve their skills. This is another way to rapidly get the new employee integrated into the culture.

Endnotes

1. The article is titled "5 Powerful Steps To Improve Employee Engagement" by Brent Gleeson, dated October 15, 2017; https://www.forbes.com/sites/brentgleeson/2017/10/15/5-powerful-steps-to-improve-employee-engagement/#2e2dd6f6341d; accessed August 13, 2018.

2. Ibid.

3. Ibid.

Chapter 8

GREAT LEADERS
ENGAGE

**You Can Build an Engaged Team of Highly
Motivated and Productive Team Members.**

If you're like me, you've probably grown just a little bit tired of all the articles about millennials in the workplace. It seems like every day I see ten new headlines about how younger workers are taking over—and now there are even articles about Generation Z!

I understand that there is talent in all generations and there is one thing I know about great leaders, they do more than just zero in on the little distinctions that separate one generation from the next. And great leaders *never* pit generations against one another, as if to suggest one is worthier than the other.

Great leaders bring different age groups *together*—engaging them in the workplace, fostering a spirit of inclusion, celebrating differences and affirming common purpose.

Obviously, that's a mouthful—but how is it done?

Here are a few ways you can improve your skills when engaging across different age groups:

 Define your culture in terms of behaviors and values, not age. Your employees may think that age disparity is a big deal—but what if you define each job and each project in terms of specific behaviors and values? Then, all of a sudden, age is less of an issue. Employees either have the values you're looking for or they don't, and age has nothing to do with it.

 Give the gift of your feedback. No matter the employee's age, rest assured that he or she craves your feedback—affirmation for good work, timely and specific critiques for subpar work. Don't scrimp on feedback because you think an employee is too young to handle it or too old to need it!

⊛ **Allow employees to provide their feedback.** Engaging employees means doing more than just telling them what to do. Engaging leaders also provide specific forums for team members to offer suggestions and input on how the team is functioning.

⊛ **Provide training where needed.** Some employees—older ones, in particular—may be unengaged because they fear they lack the necessary skillsets to contribute to the team. Support all team members by providing training and instruction where needed.

⊛ **Support mentorship programs.** Another great way to promote unity on your team is to create a formal mentorship program—pair older and younger employees and let them encourage one another.

There is a term that I use called Tribal Knowledge. This is the information that certain employees who have had years of experience on the job possess, but you can only learn it by putting in the time. When this information is passed down in a mentorship or mastermind meeting, the company and the team will grow exponentially, and engagement will begin to increase.

That's just one way successful leaders can begin to build their teams. Next, let's look at a few of the habits of highly engaging leaders.

Five Habits of Highly Engaging Leaders

So much of life comes down to the habits that we form. Want to be healthy and physically fit? It's all about developing the right habits for eating and exercise. Want to have stronger relationships? Get into the habit of connecting, communicating, and showing others your affection.

And if you want to be a more engaging leader—well, there are some habits to form for that, too. I recommend these five, in particular:

1. **Plan to engage.** It's difficult to be engaging when you're making everything up as you go along. Of course, you may find yourself in unexpected situations with surprise opportunities to talk to employees or to potential customers, but most of the time you will have time to plan ahead. Want to run an engaging team meeting? Take time to plan your approach before the meeting. Want to engage a new client, rather than bore him to death? Plan your pitch in advance.

2. **Listen.** Get into the habit of understanding before you try to make yourself understood. This means getting out of the habit of talking over other people or struggling to assert your point of view first and last. Make sure you always take time to figure out where other people are coming from.

3. **Think win-win.** One of the best ways to engage people is to present your case in a win-win manner—explaining not just why you want a given outcome, but why it's also good for the other person. Be proactive about it; force yourself to always think win-win, and to lay out benefits and values.

4. **Focus on the outcome.** Always know what kind of outcome you want to achieve, and lead with it. Whether you're talking to a customer or a team member, be

upfront about what you hope to achieve. This gives your conversations direction.

5. **Follow-up.** Engagement is a two-way street—and while I don't necessarily think you need to micromanage, I do think you need to give people time to ask questions and offer you feedback. Get into the habit of providing time for questions and feedback, if you're not already.

It takes time and diligence to be an engaging leader—and it takes the formation of good, healthy habits. One of the things I suggest to all leaders and managers is to take a daily walk-about!

Whenever I show up at the office in the morning, I make it a habit to say hello to everyone and ask them if there's anything they need. Most of the time they just say no, everything is under control. I know that! My goal is to ensure that everyone knows I have their back. When there is something important to discuss, they will be less likely to be intimidated or afraid to share the information with me if I am consistent with this technique.

This will work well for you too. When they want your attention or help, they will feel at ease to ask for it. There are some other things that you can also do to manage and develop your future team of leaders.

Managing Employees, Developing Leaders

Employee engagement doesn't happen by accident, nor does it start with the employees themselves. If you want engagement to rise at your company, it's important to take initiative—beginning with leaders, managers, and supervisors.

If you're in a position where employees report to you directly, that means you have considerable sway over engagement. The question is, what can you do to increase that engagement? Rock stars aren't born, they are developed.

Quick-Start Ways to Improve Engagement

Make face-time a priority. Schedule daily, or at the very least weekly, huddles where you meet with your team to provide direction and field questions. This is an important way to show your investment in each employee.

Set clear expectations. Define what each person's role is, specifically, and make it clear to them how they add value and how they contribute to the overall mission.

Let your team members do what they do best. Assign projects and responsibilities based on what people are good at and what they enjoy; play to strengths as much as you can.

Listen to what your employees are saying. When team members come to you with input or suggestions, actively listen; be silent while they speak, rather than inserting yourself into the conversation. Then talk with them about what they just presented. You may not follow through on their advice or solve the issue immediately, but assure them that you heard what they had to say and value their input.

Keep everyone on the same page. Be able to clearly identify the mission and purpose of your company;

articulate it to your team regularly; and show how everything you're doing connects to the mission. Allow your team members to feel like they are part of something bigger than themselves. Engagement won't happen unless you nurture it—and that's something solutions-oriented leaders will do starting now by following these proven-successful guidelines.

A majority of the communications that take place in any organization happens in team meetings. Let's explore how we can make those meetings more effective and engaging.

Improve Engagement and Save Time

Are you *wasting time* in your team meetings? I asked that very question in a recent blog post and have been surprised by the number of managers and leaders who have approached me upon reading it. Some responses were similar: "I never realized just how wasteful my meetings were. But what can I possibly do to make my meetings more productive?"

If this sounds like your response, one thing you might consider is that some meetings may not be necessary at all. In the American workplace, we sometimes confuse *meetings* with *getting things done*—but as I've mentioned elsewhere in this book, if you can't quickly and easily articulate the reason and goal of your meeting, then it probably doesn't need to be held.

Beyond that, let me offer a simple, though not *easy*, strategy for making your meetings more meaningful—*engage your team members*. If they're actually involved with what you're discussing on every level— if they're not just hearing but actually *listening* and contributing as well—then every minute you spend in that meeting is going to be, on some level, valuable.

Of course, you don't just wave a wand to make engagement materialize in the hearts and minds of your team members. It's not that easy. Building engagement takes some time and some effort—but with the right strategies, it's possible!

Making Your Meetings More Engaging

So how do you do it? Let me offer some quick pointers:

Frame your meeting as a chance to solve problems. Meetings that lack focus will also lack engagement. But what if you state the *specific* problem that your team is facing, and ask for suggestions for improvement?

Start with something positive. Before you get into problems and solutions, talk about what's going right for your team—or ask team members for some reflections on what *they* think is going right.

Encourage everyone to participate. You might go around the room and ask everyone to voice an idea— no matter how big or small, how rough or how precise. Just be comfortable with a few moments of silence as people think—and remember to be supportive of all ideas voiced! There's no room for harsh criticism in a brainstorming session.

Break down into groups. Divide your team into sub-teams of two or three people and have them brainstorm together before reporting back to the group.

Show respect. I can't say it enough. If you want your team members to be engaged in your meetings, you have to convince them that their ideas will be respected, not mocked, dismissed, or picked apart right in front of them!

Have an agenda. The number-one reason that I've seen as a cause for wasteful meetings is lack of an agenda. Without an agenda there is generally no purpose or direction for the meeting and most people will be unprepared.

Productive meetings *are* possible—and they start with a detailed agenda, specific timelines, and engagement strategies built in for all involved.

There are three things that can sabotage employee engagement, and many times each rears its ugly head in team meetings. Let's look at those right now.

Three Ways to Self-Sabotage Engagement

There's nothing in your company culture that doesn't have an impact on employee engagement. Every ritual, every rule, every practice affects employee engagement in some way—whether for good or for ill. As such, even team leaders who have the best intentions can inadvertently undercut their own attempts to keep employees motivated.

The following are three of the most common forms of self-sabotage.

1. Micromanaging

You hired your team members for a reason—ostensibly because you believe in them and trust them to do a good job.

Your employees need to be reminded of this. They need to have you affirm it to them, both in word and in action. But when you delegate something to them and then lean over their shoulder, not allowing them the freedom to accomplish anything on their own terms, you undermine that message. In doing so, you can sabotage employee confidence.

Simply put, you have to trust your people. And if you don't, you shouldn't have hired them in the first place.

2. Blaming Your Employees

Everyone makes mistakes. In fact, that's one of the main ways in which we grow. But if you jump on your employees for every little error, casting blame rather than offering support, you suppress that growth potential.

There is a time and a place for constructive criticism—but if blame is all you offer, don't be shocked when employee engagement tanks.

3. Not Giving Enough Credit

Your team should rise and fall *together;* you share victories as well as defeats. And if the team accomplishes something, everyone should feel good about it.

Don't take all the credit for yourself. Don't deprive your employees of the affirmation they deserve after a job well done. Make sure everyone feels included in your company's broader sense of mission—and in the achievement of key objectives.

Engagement Surveys

Employee engagement should emanate from all corners of your company—and that starts by recognizing the areas where you're coming up short. If you're aware of these problems in your company, take action against them today!

One of the best ways to discover what's working and what's not is by investing your time in periodic employee engagement surveys.

The *employee engagement survey* has long been a staple of culture-savvy businesses—and for good reason!

Engagement is key to employee productivity, morale, and retention—in short, good for the bottom line. And when it comes to taking the pulse on employee engagement, regularly checking in with employees to see how they're doing, an engagement survey is really a no-brainer.

As a leadership speaker, I visit a lot of companies that conduct annual or semi-regular employee engagement surveys. I know that business leaders and HR executives see the value in these surveys—but sometimes, they don't know exactly what they should be asking. They worry that their surveys aren't providing them the kind of insights they need.

It's all too easy to ask the wrong survey questions when you don't *truly* understand what motivates employees. So that's a good starting point—to nail your employee engagement survey, you have to understand where engagement really comes from. Study after study confirms that engagement is locked into three basic concepts:

- Employees who understand their role and their fit within the broader organization;

- Employees who think they learn in the workplace, and develop their professional skillsets; and

- Employees who feel empowered to address challenges and changes in the workplace.

Asking the Right Questions

When you understand these three drivers of employee engagement, you can begin to formulate survey questions that really get to the heart of the matter. Here are a few examples of effective employee engagement survey questions:

- Do you understand the company's mission and strategic goals?

- Do you know what you should do to help the company meet its mission and goals?

- Do you see the connection between your work and the company's broader mission and goals?

- Does your team inspire you to do your very best work?

- Do you have access to the information and tools you need to make correct decisions in the workplace?

- When an unexpected problem arises, do you know who to ask for help?

Happiness Quotient

I also ask survey questions revolving around happiness. What's important to them at work? It's the little things that make the big difference, and if you don't ASK you won't GET!

After you have this valuable information, you can act on it and adapt it into your company culture.

Your first challenge is to diagnose your company culture and understand it before you can build an engaged team of highly motivated and productive team members.

Chapter 9

DEVELOPING YOUR
CULTURE

**Create Your Own Corporate Culture That Enables
You, Your Company, and Your Team to Grow.**

I have been blessed in my life to have had the opportunity to work with many different companies around the world, delivering training programs, executive coaching, and keynote speeches. This has enabled me to learn many lessons from some of the top company leaders in the world about what it takes to lead, engage, and grow business.

However, there is one company that stands out in my mind and in the industry that they serve. I absolutely love to work with people who truly walk their talk—and it starts from the top down!

That company is Ultimate Software, and I have had the privilege of speaking at a number of their human resource workshops around the country. If a company is going to make a cultural change that grows their business and takes care of their employees and clients, there is no better company than Ultimate Software to emulate. Year after year the leadership continues to innovate, evolve, and engage their employees and clients.

In fact, when you go to the Ultimate Software website, there is a section specifically explaining the company culture, which states that their commitment is to people, their community, and their culture.

The mantra of the company is "People First" and that trickle-down effect comes from the top! Many companies place their mission and vision statement on their website and in their office; however, few companies truly live that mission and vision, and even fewer employees even know the mission or vision of their own company. Scott Scherr founded Ultimate Software in 1990 and has served as president and CEO since the company's inception. His goal is to continuously innovate and strive for product excellence while fostering a culture based on honesty and respect, which is his number-one priority.

No, I've never had the pleasure of meeting Scott; however, having worked with his team in multiple locations across the United States, I can tell you that they speak in glowing terms of him as a person and a solutions-oriented leader.

The human resource workshops that Ultimate Software presents are first-class productions and delivered at no charge for existing clients and other HR professionals who may be interested in attending. The attendees can view some of the best HR software in the world and learn how it will help them in their business. Attendees hear world-class speakers who deliver valuable and timely information that will immediately help them perform at a higher level. And as a major value-added item, as if the presentations are not enough, all attendees receive a delicious breakfast and lunch in addition to receiving the continuing education hours required to maintain their license.

It's no wonder that every year Ultimate Software moves up in the rankings on many different lists. The following is a list of some of the awards earned in 2018:

- Ranked #1 on *Fortune's* Best Workplace for Millennial's list

- Ranked #1 on *CIO.com's* 10 Best Places to Work for Women in Technology list

- Ranked #1 on *Computerworld's* Best Place to Work in IT Among Midsize Organizations list

- Ranked #2 on *Glassdoor's* 25 Highest Rated Public Cloud Computing Companies to Work list

- Ranked #1 on *Fortune's* Best Workplaces and Technology list

And climbing the ranks from #7 in 2017 to #3 in 2018 on *Fortune's* 2018 Best Place to Work list

Ultimate Software is led by an amazing team of professionals with whom I have had the privilege to work, including Leslie Berke, Molly Bushwaller, Phillipa Stephenson, Jody Piper, Jill L. Risse, and two of my favorite people on the planet, Tony Segreto and Joey Cornblit. Their focus on *people first* is ingrained in their corporate culture and the common thread that is embraced by the whole Ultimate Software family that continues to make them solutions-oriented leaders in their industry.

Let's see how we can implement just some of the lessons in the next chapters and you can create your own corporate culture that enables you, your company, and your team to grow.

Describing Your Company Culture

If you had to describe your company culture in one word, what word would you choose?

And don't cheat by saying just *good* or *bad*. Think more descriptively. How would you diagnose the fundamental character of your team, your office environment, your company's values?

Knowing what kind of company culture you have can be invaluable as you try to determine what works and what doesn't for your team, and how well your organizational values align with your corporate mission. It helps you know where your strengths are and where you might make improvements.

No two company cultures are ever quite the same, of course, but there are some useful general words and concepts when diagnosing cultural basics. Which of these words, if any, reflects *your* workplace culture?

- **Collaborative.** In your office environment, do team members band together in open dialogue? Is there an attitude of shared ownership and a passion for problem-solving? Or are your team members isolated and insular, working privately and not together?

- **Creative.** Would you characterize your workspace as one in which innovation is valued and fostered? Do your team members feel comfortable bringing up new ideas or experimenting with the way things are done—or do they all adhere to tradition, to "the way we've always done things"?

- **Controlled.** Do you have an extremely formal, rules-based workplace—do people feel like they have to do things a certain way or face dire consequences? Does your workplace emphasize dependability and hierarchical authority?

- **Competitive.** Are your team members working to outdo one another, to bring in the best results on the company's behalf? Is there a "survival of the fittest" mentality in your workplace culture? Is your organization unified by a zeal for winning, however you may define that term?

There are many different kinds of company cultures—but what cultural style best epitomizes your business? Are you comfortable with the diagnosis—or is it time to initiate cultural change? As I noted earlier, Stephen Covey advises, "Begin with the end in mind," which always starts with self-analysis and asking yourself questions that will help you build and improve your team!

Seven Keys to Building Your Team and Encouraging Teamwork

Great teams don't happen by accident. There are several components that you need to have in place for a great team to emerge. You need to have a vision for everyone to rally behind. You need to have a leader who fosters and encourages *teamwork and collaboration*. And crucially, you need a work environment that is conducive to working *together* toward a shared goal.

This last point is one that a lot of companies are starting to pay attention to and rethink conventions. Consider the "open office" phenomenon. Consider the number of companies that believe you have to have a big, fun campus like Google's in order to have a truly coherent and effective team.

Your office environment can certainly have an impact on team dynamics, but it's not the most important thing. The more important thing is your company culture that's reflected in how you lead, how you manage, how you arrange your office, how you communicate with your team, and more.

The question is, how do you develop an organizational culture that sparks true teamwork and camaraderie? Here are seven keys to success:

1. The first thing to remember is that, as I've noted previously, great teamwork begins with, well, a great *team*. What I mean by that is that you lay the foundations for

great teamwork simply by assembling a team of individuals who fit in with your company culture and values, and who bring diverse and complementary skills to the table.

2. Communication is, as ever, the key. Quiet teams are usually not very productive or unified teams. That doesn't mean you have to plan a corporate getaway or a team-building activity every day of the week; but do plan ten or fifteen minutes each day just to get everyone together to discuss the team's goals and progress.

3. Implicit in the previous step is making sure your employees all know what the team goals are. Make sure there is a road map of where things are headed, and that you communicate how everyone fits in on that journey.

4. Set clear, measurable goals both for the team overall and for individuals. Make those goals challenging, but attainable—and make sure you offer recognition and affirmation when goals are met!

5. Try to avoid anything that stands in the way of effective, two-way dialogue. Everyone on the team should feel comfortable offering thoughts, opinions, and critiques. If there is fear about speaking up or speaking out, you have a problem you need to address.

6. Work to correct performance issues promptly and privately. A team member who clashes with others or doesn't understand the team goals may just need a little extra counseling or communication.

7. Finally, remember that teamwork begins with the leader of the company. Lead by example. Communicate

openly, be accepting of feedback, cherish other voices and opinions, and solicit help when you need it!

Building a great team requires strategy and real leadership. However, one of the determining factors of all championship teams and organizations is self-confidence. Self-confidence is powerful.

As automobile business magnate Henry Ford said, "Whether you think you can, or you think you can't—you're right."

Does Your Culture Give Employees Confidence?

Would you like to have employees who are bold in their decision-making, strong in their convictions, and empowered to do what they think is right—to truly give you their best work and their highest level of effort, day in and day out?

Or would you rather have employees who are chronically unsure, uncertain, and wishy-washy—never wanting to do anything decisive without you giving them the green light or offering to hold their hand?

Most leaders would prefer the former, and it's not hard to understand why. Having a true team means having employees who feel confident in contributing and in using the talents and gifts that made you hire them in the first place.

John Leone is a solutions-oriented leader. He is one of the owners of International Liquors Tobacco and Trading (ILTT) and Heineken in St. Maarten, an island in the Caribbean Sea. He has always had his hand on the pulse of his employees, with a focus on family first and delivering world-class customer service.

When Hurricane Irma made a direct hit on St. Maarten on September 6, 2017, John's house was completely destroyed. His wife, Wendy, and their three boys huddled in the concrete basement, the only portion remaining of their home after the storm.

John told me he had backup plan after backup plan in case of an emergency on the island. But Irma was devastating. When asked what he was going to do, he told everyone he was going to rebuild! John told me the one thing he had to do was believe he could rebuild his house and his life. If he was ever going to convince his family and his employees, he had to believe it himself.

John collected everything they owned and could salvage, but most of their personal belongings were destroyed. John then made it a priority to share resources with neighbors, salvaging materials from around the island, including his own generator.

He used one of the generators to help his friend John Caputo, owner of Domino's Pizza on St. Maarten, to get his operation going again after it was destroyed in the hurricane. The generator John salvaged helped his friend get his business up and running, which enabled him to feed the first responders and the people on the island.

John also secured 100,000 liters of water for distribution to the people of St. Maarten as a contribution from Heineken.

The most common question everyone asked John, "Would the 39th Heineken Regatta take place in St. Maarten this year?" Six days after Irma, John Leone decided that the regatta would move forward. This decision gave the people of St. Maarten hope—and his team a goal to focus on.

Being a solutions-oriented leader who focuses on results, John used the Heineken Regatta as a fundraiser to help foundations rebuild the island. John even cowrote a song and produced a music video with the band Orange Grove to help raise money for the people and businesses affected.

John's mantra to his employees: ***Be Positive, Be Patient, Be Smart, and Family First!*** When he says this, his employees look at him and ask if he's okay, because they know if John Leone is okay, they will be okay too!

That's what creating a culture of confidence looks like!

Where Does Culture Enter the Equation?

But would you believe that, to a large extent, your company culture decides whether employees act confidently or hesitantly? It's true. Your workplace values and vision can go a long way toward either cultivating or undermining employee confidence.

So, if you want to establish a culture that creates confidence, you may want to consider the following tips:

 Help your employees build awareness of their strengths. The more comfortable they are identifying their own strong points, the more confidence they'll have acting on those strong points. In particular, you can encourage reflection and journaling, asking employees to spend time thinking about the workplace activities that most energize them; you can also share positive gleanings from your own performance reviews, or peer performance reviews.

Brainstorm ways to make those strengths even more productive. Speak with employees about their strengths, encouraging them to go beyond self-awareness. Ask them to work with you to discover different ways their strengths can add value to the office.

Give praise where praise is due. Always offer public affirmation and gratitude for significant achievements—letting employees know that their good work is not just noticed but appreciated.

Offer constructive feedback. You can and should share ways your employees can improve, but make sure to balance the bad with the good and offer specific ways they can do so. Do not give just vague criticisms or disapprovals.

Lead by example. Whatever you do, don't spend time beating yourself up or publicly harping on your own shortcomings. Recognize the ways in which you need to improve, then move on! Ultimately, building a culture of confidence starts with you, the leader! Teams go where you go! When you show up to work, you are on stage and everyone expects a perfect performance. When you become a solutions-oriented leader, you will have a team of solutions-oriented employees.

It's also important for you to have, as Zig Ziglar would say, "A checkup, from the neck up." It's important for you as a leader to develop cultural feedback so you have your hand on the pulse of your team to take them to the next level.

Feedback is gold, so let's see why!

Do You Have a Feedback Culture?

Leader, I have a couple of important questions for you: "Do you actively court feedback? Are you constantly seeking insight into how you're doing your job, and suggestions for how you could do it even better?"

To ask even more pointedly, "If one of your team members approached you with a constructive performance review, how would you take it?" Would you get defensive? Would you get angry? Or would you welcome it for what it was—an invaluable opportunity to become sharper, stronger, and more effective as a leader?

See, we all like to receive praise and affirmation, but none of us particularly like being told we have room for improvement. That's especially true when the constructive criticism comes from someone who is "under" us. But that feedback shouldn't be viewed as a personal affront. We shouldn't be insulted by it. Actually, we should soak it up. We should scramble for any chance we get to become even *better* at what we do.

Everyone has blind spots—parts of our behavior that we may not see so clearly. Feedback helps us identify those areas, to see ourselves as others see us. That can be painful, but it can also be a road map, pointing us down avenues for improvement.

A smart solutions-oriented leader welcomes any and all feedback. Not only that, but he or she works to create a company culture in which feedback flows freely and everyone craves chances for improvement. The question is, how can you do this?

Let me offer just a few quick suggestions:

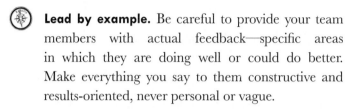 **Lead by example.** Be careful to provide your team members with actual feedback—specific areas in which they are doing well or could do better. Make everything you say to them constructive and results-oriented, never personal or vague.

Have an open-door policy. Make it clear to your team members that you're always around and welcome any input they may have.

Respond appropriately. Remember, if you're going to tell people you care about their input, you can't be defensive when they tell you things you don't want to hear. Listen and acknowledge whatever feedback comes your way.

Have a formalized feedback process. Make sure you have regular performance reviews; don't just provide employees with feedback, also give them a chance to offer you feedback.

Take it to the customers. Look outside your team for potential feedback or suggestions. Send out customer surveys. Let your clients know you care about their experience and listen to what they have to say.

Building a feedback culture may take some time and may leave you feeling a little bit bruised along the way—but it's ultimately worth it as you seek to make your leadership as effective as possible.

Sometimes the truth hurts, but if you want results, if you want to be the best you can be, feedback is essential especially with younger employees.

Younger Employees Value Culture

Young employees value culture—and you should, too. Leader, are you paying attention to the younger employees on your team—members of the so-called millennial generation, in particular?

I occasionally see comments that are dismissive of these younger workers—alleging that they are too tech-obsessed, they are always glued to their phone, or what have you—but in my experience none of the common complaints about millennials actually hold true. These folks are usually sharp and substantive, as far as I can tell—and that's a good thing. As of last year, they represent the single largest generational demographic in the workforce.

They are not going anywhere, either, so it's important to try to understand what drives them. What drives members of this generation may be different from what drives older employees. As mentioned previously, most millennials aren't just working for a paycheck. *What they're after is a richer array of benefits* including a flexible work environment, opportunities to learn and develop themselves, and companies that have a distinct vision and invite employees to be part of it.

In other words, what millennials want is *culture*.

There are a variety of explanations for this. First, millennials came of age during the Great Recession (2007-2010), and as such they know how tenuous employment can be. Chances for professional growth and development matter nearly as much as a steady paycheck; then, even if the paycheck goes away, the skills mastered can be carried over into a new position.

Meanwhile, the consumer environment in which millennials have grown up places a clear premium on ideas over tangible goods.

Think about how the vision and ethos of Airbnb, Uber, and even tech companies like Google have united people, providing a sense of belonging and social engagement.

There are a few takeaways from all this information about young employees and company culture. First and foremost, if you want to recruit top talents from this critical demographic, you have to offer more than the standard salary-and-benefits package. You have to offer a *culture* where they feel they belong. You have to invest in them.

And even if you don't hire any young folks any time soon, you can take a page out of their playbook. Remember that there is more to your company than what you see with your own two eyes. Some of the things that mark a company's culture are esoteric, even unexplainable—yet so important to what makes that company unique. Employees know it, consumers know it—and hopefully, you know it too!

Many times I'm asked, "Is there a way to measure my company culture just like I measure productivity?" The answer is "Yes." Let's take a look at how we can do that.

Chapter 10

MEASURING
COMPANY CULTURE

**Few Things are More Precious Than
a Great Workplace Culture.**

157

It's important to have goals, but goals don't mean much if you have no way of tracking your progress. I think that's the problem a lot of business leaders have with company culture. It's not that they don't understand it or that they don't see the merit in making cultural improvements. Often, though, they struggle to know whether their efforts are *working*—whether their culture is really improving at all.

It's a hard thing to measure, yet not impossible. In fact, there are several key metrics you can use to track the evolution of your corporate culture.

A few of those metrics include: communication, collaboration, innovation, wellness, support, and customer service. Let's look at each a bit more closely.

 Communication. Are all of your employees on the same page regarding your company's mission and values? Do you find that your current communication channels are effective, or are there frequent communication breakdowns in your company? Are conflicts common? Are they dealt with effectively when they arise? Culture fosters clear communication—and if you see obvious communication flaws, that's a sign that there's still work to be done in culture building!

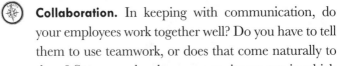 **Collaboration.** In keeping with communication, do your employees work together well? Do you have to tell them to use teamwork, or does that come naturally to them? Strong work cultures are environments in which teams flourish and people work together in unity.

 Innovation. What's the last great idea your team developed? Are you all adept at thinking outside the box? Great culture lends itself to innovation and creates an atmosphere in which everyone feels comfortable offering bold ideas for consideration.

Wellness. Are your employees physically fit and mentally able—or are they constantly stressed out or burned out? Do your employees take a lot of sick time? Are they generally sluggish or inefficient? If your team members are unhealthy, there's a good chance that your culture is, too.

Support. Do your employees think you support them? Do they know you're looking out for them, for their families, for their futures? In a healthy company culture, your employees will believe they have all the resources and support they need to thrive!

Customer service. Healthy company culture creates an environment in which customer service is a priority. If your culture is getting better, your customers should be getting happier! The bottom line for business leaders is that culture is worth investing in—and there are absolutely some ways to track your investment's progress!

Unfortunately, there are times when our metrics give us bad news and reveal that the culture is toxic. There are ways we can diagnose that and make some changes in the right direction.

Diagnosing a Toxic Work Culture

Few things are more precious than a great workplace culture.

Studies show that many employees—especially millennials—will actually settle for lower pay if it means working within a better, *more positive culture.* And as such, it's no surprise to see so many companies boasting of their cultural excellence.

But let's be real, not every workplace culture is ideal. A few are actually downright toxic—and it's important to know and be aware of that as a leader. Step back and look at your company as if you are a new applicant. And before taking a new position, make sure you're not stepping into an unpleasant cultural situation. If you already have worked in a toxic work environment, you will have some unpleasant reference points for comparison.

It all starts with a simple diagnosis. I offer the following ways to diagnose your culture based on my experience.

It's not about surface-level stuff. As a leadership coach, I've worked with businesses that have ping-pong tables, massage chairs, smoothie makers, and all kinds of other goodies. All of that's fine, and in fact it can be meaningful, but ultimately it doesn't say much about the underlying culture.

Those things are all superficial trappings. If it was that easy to *make your culture great*, every business would have great culture. Be ready to look past these surface features.

Use your senses. Instead of focusing on the outward trappings, pause to consider the workplace more deeply. Start by surveying the layout. Does it feel open and collaborative—or is everyone's workspace sequestered and secretive? That tells you a lot about the workplace culture right there.

Also, keep your eyes and ears open. How do people sound? Do the employees strike you as enthusiastic? As positive? Or as jittery and nervous? These aspects can be very revealing.

What about recruiting? Be mindful of the recruiting process. How is it paced? A good company culture will manifest itself in plenty of due diligence, ensuring that the person hired is the right fit.

Meanwhile, if there is no due diligence—and if the entire process feels rushed and reckless—that's a big red flag. Look at past employees who were let go. In hindsight, do you see any red flags in the process when they were hired?

Of course, these are just a few ways you can sort through a company culture and try to make sense of it. Even more important is your willingness to ask legitimately tough questions about your company's values and how those values are carried out day to day. Most important of all, trust your gut and if any part of your company's culture just *feels off,* get to the bottom of it quickly and correct it.

As a leader, if you are looking at your culture from a new applicant's point of view and you notice these red flags, it's time to make some changes based on your diagnosis.

One of the other elements to evaluate that contributes to a toxic culture is an environment of blame. Great leaders accept responsibility and avoid the blame game. Here's why.

Avoiding a Culture of Blame

Everybody makes mistakes, and everybody fails from time to time. What's important is that we *redeem* those failures. What's important is that we *learn* from them.

So, let me ask you, "Do your team members learn from their failures? Do you learn from yours?"

Too often the answer to these questions is, "No." That's because many corporate cultures do not make it safe to fail. Failure is met with blame, if not outright shame—which means nobody feels comfortable taking risks and nobody is willing to own up to their errors and learn from them.

That's no way to run a business. Smart, solutions-oriented leaders create environments in which employees can use their failures to *get better, to improve.*

And that means shifting away from the blame game.

Easier said than done, right? Well, not necessarily. You may have a culture of blame right now, but that doesn't mean there aren't steps you can take to improve things and create an environment where failure is safe.

Some tips for moving past a culture of blame:

- Provide your team with room to problem solve. Train them to identify issues and strategically think through potential fixes.

- Be open to suggestions for possible improvements. Don't take it as criticism; take it as meaningful feedback.

- Show real leadership by publicly acknowledging your own errors and mistakes. Don't try to hide them or cover them up. Own up to them!

- When chastising employees or discussing their shortcomings, do so in a private environment—but offer praise and affirmation publicly.

Remind your team members that failures and mistakes are learning opportunities and encourage your team members to pause and reflect on what they can learn from their own shortcomings.

The blame game wastes time and prevents you from really *using* your failures. It's worth your while to create a culture in which blame never enters the picture.

Remember that the Baseball Hall of Fame players who have a lifetime batting average of 300 struck out 70 percent of the time. The key is to fail fast, accept responsibility, and remain curious!

How to Build a Culture of Curiosity

Sometimes I feel like we've got the concept of curiosity all wrong. You know the old saying: Curiosity killed the cat. There's a very real sense in which our culture is wary of those who are open-minded, eager to learn new things or seek out new concepts. But I think that's all wrong. As a leadership speaker, I have encountered a number of businesses where curiosity is hardwired into the culture—and that only ever yields good things.

What makes curiosity so beneficial? For one thing, curious employees are engaged employees. Being open to new ideas and experiences leads to career enrichment, personal satisfaction, and a relentless hunger to do and learn more; when you're curious, you can't be complacent! Plus, those who are curious are always expanding their skillsets, often in ways that can make the entire team stronger, more dynamic.

I encourage business owners and managers to cultivate cultures of curiosity—but how? Let me offer some quick suggestions.

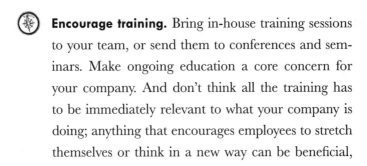

Encourage training. Bring in-house training sessions to your team, or send them to conferences and seminars. Make ongoing education a core concern for your company. And don't think all the training has to be immediately relevant to what your company is doing; anything that encourages employees to stretch themselves or think in a new way can be beneficial, even if you can't immediately see how.

Foster collaboration. Ensure that your employees are constantly working together in different partnerships and configurations; really encourage cross-discipline and cross-department teamwork. Allow your employees to be exposed to all the different talents and gifts represented on your team.

Give ownership. Be forthright in sharing the broader company vision with your team members—and solicit their feedback. Let them know they have a say in where the business is headed. Encourage them to think bigger than their immediate tasks or daily responsibilities. Curiosity is worth striving for—and possible to attain. Consider making it one of the central values of your business!

Gamification. Turn projects and goals into games where everybody competes, and everyone wins, leading to a rock star celebration. Almost everyone loves games, and if you can align games with your goals, curiosity will flourish and productivity will increase.

Five Ways to Create a Culture of Productivity

Leader, let me invite you to step back and take an honest appraisal of your company culture. Do you find there's a lot of wasted time by your team members—including *you?* Do you feel frustrated simply trying to get people to get some work done? Do you, personally, find your office environment to be a place where it's easy to get distracted, hard to buckle down, and seemingly impossible to accomplish anything?

If you answered yes to any of those questions, then clearly, you have a problem with productivity. Don't panic. It's a fixable problem. The trick is to be *intentional* in building a culture where productivity is *ingrained.*

Building productivity into your culture isn't something you can do overnight, and frankly it's a task I recommend you tackle alongside a coach or consultant. For today, though, I can offer you a few quick tips for building a productivity culture:

1. **Share your vision.** The secret to productivity isn't you being a relentless taskmaster. It's you creating a broader sense of purpose—providing a clear objective and showing your team members how they fit into it. Be clear and unambiguous about what your company's mission is and about how each employee's role helps the team achieve that mission.

2. **Be clear about different roles.** Every team member should have a clear sense of responsibility and of the scope of his or her duties. Impart to each team member the specific value that he or she brings to the whole.

3. **Provide opportunities for growth and development.** Over time, employees may grow a little tired or bored in their role, which is when productivity can slack off. Make sure you provide plenty of ways for employees to reach for the next thing—to improve their professional skillsets and take on greater challenges. Formal training programs can be especially valuable!

4. **Provide regular feedback.** To have a culture of productivity you also need a culture of feedback. Have formal channels for appraising your team members' work, including a regular employee review cycle. Everyone wants feedback!

5. **Facilitate collaboration.** Team members will work harder when you allow them to work together. Make sure you assign big projects to groups, not individuals, and provide a space that lends itself to collaborative work.

Make productivity part of your culture—and start by showing your team members how they fit into the big picture and how they benefit. Most importantly your employees want to feel like rock stars and know they are valued. That doesn't always mean you have to spend more money.

Affordable Ways to Show Employees You Care

Here's a question: If you had a job where you didn't feel valued or appreciated—where you felt like you couldn't make a difference and that your efforts were going unnoticed—how long would you stick around at that job? It's a no-brainer. You wouldn't stay around any longer than necessary. You'd bolt at the first chance to land a job where you *would* feel valued.

And guess what? Your employees feel the same way. That's why one of the most important jobs that HR professionals and small business owners face is ensuring that their employees *know* how valued they are.

And maybe you really *do* value your employees, but have a hard time proving it—for reasons that boil down to your budget. You can always make employees feel valued by giving them huge raises, but that's just not an affordable solution. So, the question is, how can you show value *without* blowing your budget?

The following suggestions are not necessarily free, but they are low cost and potentially high impact—meaning they can be smart ways to boost your employee retention.

Innovation Days: Take a couple of days out of each year to let your employees step away from their normal responsibilities to address projects to improve office efficiencies, create a better work environment, brainstorm strategies for the company's future, or otherwise exhibit their input and their passion.

Service Days: Provide employees with a couple of (paid) days each year when they can leave the office to participate in a charity or volunteer project that means something to them—proving that you really care about the things your employees care about.

Stock the Kitchen: This is almost a cliché by now, but it's a cliché because it works. Show your employees that you care about their commitment to the office—the least you can do is offer free coffee, soft drinks, or healthy snacks.

Team Lunches: Whether monthly or quarterly, offer to buy everyone lunch in order to encourage bonding time and company fellowship.

Commuter Benefits: For employees who travel great distances, offer a monthly stipend to help offset costs.

Flexible Work Hours: Provide employees with greater leeway in when they do their work—thus allowing them to tailor their schedules to their other interests.

Paid Time Off (PTO) flexibility: Why would you care whether employees use their PTO for sick days, vacation, or simply personal time? Be flexible and non-discriminating when possible, understanding that there will be times when everyone in the company will have to be ready and available during certain times of the year.

Sabbaticals: What if every five years, an employee received a paid week off from work? That could really help employees feel valued over the long haul.

These few ideas are really just the tip of the iceberg. But here's a final secret—your employees will appreciate your effort. Whatever you can do to show you care won't go unnoticed or ignored. And when you make an effort, you shouldn't be surprised when employees return it.

Employees will stay with you longer if they like you. Do your best to have a high likability factor and your retention rate will also increase. To build a solutions-oriented culture you're going to have to undertake a self-transformation.

Chapter 11

HOW TO HANDLE
CHANGE

**When change happens,
How Will I Respond to It?**

This chapter title was initially, "Learn How to Handle Change—or, Are You Still Using Your Blackberry?" I was told it was too lengthy for a chapter title, but I'm sure you get my point regarding how changes can be tough in any area of life.

Change is one of the few certainties in the business world—and generally, in life. The question that successful people ask isn't whether or not things will change. The million-dollar question is, *When change happens, how will I respond to it?*

You see, good, solutions-oriented leaders can weather change—survive it. Great leaders thrive on change. They see every fork in the road or ebb in the tide as an opportunity to learn something, to develop their business, and to get better at what they do.

There are a number of ways that I found to be helpful in responding to change constructively:

 Never take it personally. Understand that change is the cost of doing business. Even if your star manager or your favorite sales leader abruptly quits, or a big client withdraws a large order for no apparent reason, remember that it's just business. There's no use in allowing it to hurt your feelings.

 Be candid about it. Pretending like change isn't happening is a mistake, if only because your team members will think you're being too insular or cutting them out of the loop. Be transparent about the change that's going on at your company in order to prevent employee confusion.

 Stay positive. Even with a really unwelcome change, there is often a silver lining—a chance for you to learn a new skill, bring in a great new employee, or watch as other team members rise to meet new challenges.

Focus on these positives, rather than letting the negatives crush your morale.

 Start planning. Instead of reacting to change—based on your emotions or your impulses—*respond* to it, thoughtfully and constructively. Formulate a plan to guide you and your team through the change, capitalizing on it however you can.

Change is inevitable, and how you respond to it is the key to your success as a leader. We react from emotion and respond from intellect. It's not easy because we are all human, but how you handle it as a leader determines how your team responds to change.

How to Change Your Team's Behavior

There's an old saying: *Hire behaviors, train skills.* Even for those employers who live by this adage and hire team members based on their cultural fit, there may be the occasional behavioral issue on your team. It doesn't even have to be that people are behaving badly; sometimes they're just not quite aligned with the values or productivity model you strive to uphold.

Less than stellar behavior is nothing to panic about; it's natural for employees to fall into ruts or to develop little habits that you'd rather break. And as a leader, there are some simple steps you can take to bring about positive change.

Start with Numbers

The first thing you should do is to measure the behaviors you're trying to change—quantifying them, if at all possible. For instance, say you have a problem with tardiness. Keep a record of how many employees are tardy over a given span of time; you can convert that into a ratio—for instance, you might find that 15 percent of your employees are tardy to work at least three days out of each week.

Having some real data to work with, to show that you're not imagining things, is a helpful first step.

Track Progress

When you take that data to your employees, let them know their tardiness has become an issue and that you hope to see improvements. The next step is to monitor their progress. Pay attention to the employees who make an effort to improve their behavior—and perhaps even post the results to show that their good efforts have *not* gone unnoticed.

Make it clear that you're paying attention—and that you appreciate good efforts being made.

Create Consequences

Finally, hold people accountable. I don't necessarily recommend a big, sweeping statement such as, "The next person who comes in late is fired!" What I do recommend is taking note of repeat offenders and counseling them *privately* about their behavior. Work with them individually and brainstorm ways you can help them bring about that positive change in their daily behavior.

That's what this is all about—positive change. Leaders who embrace a commitment to ongoing training are leaders who experience the most positive growth.

Encouraging a Commitment to Training

As discussed previously, there are different ways in which employee training can benefit a company—through increased *retention*, through team *cohesion*, and more. But of course, I've left room for an important question. Supposing your company decides to invest in team training, *how do you get your employees on board?*

Often, it won't be as much of an uphill climb as you might anticipate. Your team members want you to invest in them. They want to learn and to develop in their professional skills. They want you to confirm for them that you plan to keep them on your team for the long haul. In many workplaces, team members really *want* training, and there's not much you'll have to do to talk them into it.

Still, you may have some skeptics and some holdouts—and if that's the case, then it becomes important for your company's leadership to cultivate real *excitement* for the training process.

The following are a few ways to generate that excitement:

 Lead by example. Attend training seminars or webinars yourself, then report back to your team on what you learned and how you think it will improve their on-the-job performance.

 Involve them in selecting the training courses. Ask your team members in which areas they would most like to receive training. You don't necessarily have to hold a democratic vote but do at least get employees involved in the conversation.

 Articulate your goals. What do you hope to get out of the training? How will it improve your team and your individual team members? Clarify your goals before the training begins.

 Ensure accountability. Are you investing in customer service training for your team? Then when the training is over, you should expect to see some improvements in customer service. Make it clear to your team that you expect them to learn, retain, and implement the new skills!

At the end of the day, you can't force anyone to be enthusiastic about training—but again, training is something that benefits your team members, and most of them are going to know it. Articulating your expectations and modeling your own enthusiasm should push everyone in the right direction.

Also, if you've done a good job in employee onboarding, there will be an expectation of ongoing training and growth. There may still be obstacles to employee training, but they can be overcome if there is a desire for improvement.

Overcoming Four Hurdles to Employee Training

Training your employees doesn't just make them more proficient in what they do, it makes them more engaged. It helps them feel more valued, and thus happier at work. It shows that you're investing in their future, and it empowers them to do their work confidently.

Most business owners know this, which is why, if you ask them, they readily agree that employee training is crucial. However, for many business owners, actually implementing employee training is a challenge. The advantages of employee training are well known, but the hurdles are significant—and on a pragmatic level, a lot of businesses just don't have the structures or procedures in place to accommodate in-house training.

But even the biggest obstacles to employee training can be overcome—as is explained in the remainder of this chapter.

What are the Most Significant Training Obstacles?

The four most frequently cited hurdles to effective training include:

1. **Time.** Some small business owners simply don't have the time to invest in training their people, which is understandable. The important thing to realize is that you don't have to provide the training *yourself*, and in fact it's often more advantageous to bring in an outsider. A few ways to mitigate the time problem include:

   Invest in webinars or in-house seminars for your team.

   Provide opportunities for certain departments or employees to attend outside conferences or workshops.

   Implement a mentor program in your workplace.

   These methods are effective and require minimal time commitment from the company leadership.

2. **Turnover.** Another major hurdle to effective training is the idea that you're going to invest in training employees only to see a number of them leave your company, taking those skills to other employers. It's certainly true that most employees will leave, sooner or later, and there's not much you can do about that—but remember that training is an investment in employee retention. By

showing your employees that you care about empowering them and developing them, you're *reducing* turnover, not courting a higher level of risk.

3. **Information overload.** Depending on your industry, you may have a lot of training needs—safety training, legal compliance, on-the-job skills, and so forth. Some business owners fear that they're burdening their employees with *too much* professional development, and that it all has an inundating effect over time. But this isn't an argument *against* training, not really. Rather, it's an argument for better prioritizing your training and ensuring that you're judicious in how you choose to develop your team.

4. **Employee diversity.** A final consideration is the fact that all employees are, well, different—and blanket approaches to training can therefore seem a bit obtuse. But that's ultimately not a great reason to avoid training, as the sheer number of training resources available today ensures that you can always calibrate your training initiative to meet the specific needs of your employees.

The old saying, "Where there's a will there's a way" applies to the importance of training as well as your desire as a leader to make it happen! If you still have not bought into the benefits of ongoing employee training, let me share with you some reasons to invest in your team.

Investing in Team Training

Most business leaders will at least pay lip service to the notion of team training—but when push comes to shove, how many are actually willing to *invest* in it?

You can talk about the benefits of training all day every day, but many business owners are reluctant to actually spend money on it. This reluctance is not ill-founded. For any business investment, it is important to see the Return On Investment (ROI), and when it comes to team training, ROI may seem a little hard to directly correlate or quantify.

It's there, though, and if you look closely you see it. You see that team training is a brilliant investment, one that can add enormous value to your company. Consider some of the following benefits that team training offers:

- Team training increases employee retention and decreases turnover. Training your team shows that you are investing directly in *them*, cultivating their talents and developing their skillsets. Employees are aware of this, and they appreciate any opportunities you give them to better themselves as professionals.

- Team training can also improve customer loyalty. A team that is well trained is a team better equipped to provide customer service with real confidence and competence—something that can only improve the customer experience.

- Team training can also lead the way to innovation. The more confidence you provide to your team members, the more you empower them and the more they will tackle problems with creativity and vigor.

- Training helps team members bond. They share the experience of training and rally behind common goals and objectives—all of which can increase team unity and cohesion.

When you invest in team training, you invest in expanding the knowledge of your team members, which ultimately makes your team more adaptive— better able to leverage the latest technologies and innovations for business growth.

What it all comes back to is engagement. Teams that are invested in through on-site training are simply going to be more engaged, and thus happier, more energetic, and more focused—all of which means team training can pay huge dividends over time!

> The next question is focused on you. How can you as a leader with a packed schedule expand your knowledge every day to stay on top of your game?

Five Habits to Expand Your Knowledge Daily

Are you growing, each and every day? Not just physically, but intellectually? Are you actually getting smarter, more knowledge-able, and more comprehensive in your understanding of the world and your place within it?

This level of personal enrichment is hard to come by, yet it can pay huge dividends—especially for working professionals. The more you learn, the more you expand your mind, the better you'll be at engaging others in conversation, in leading, and in solving problems. Thus, it's no small thing to invest some of your time in learning and mind-expansion, even if it's just a few minutes each day.

Simple Ways to Grow

And really, a few minutes each day is all it takes. If you want to learn and to grow, it's as simple as cultivating a few smart personal habits. The following five specific habits are worth pursuing:

1. **Inform yourself.** Be proactive in seeking information about the world and about your industry or niche. Make sure you read at least one newspaper—physical or online—daily. Schedule time to read the news, perhaps over morning coffee. Make sure it's a true habit, not just something you do from time to time. Also, subscribe to industry-related magazines or blogs, or read informative blogs about history, science, or whatever field interests you! Even intellectually stimulating Twitter feeds or Facebook accounts can be helpful.

2. **Read fiction.** Work 20 or 30 minutes into each day to read fiction, or just devote yourself to reading a chapter a day. Make it something you do before bed, or maybe on the train into work each morning. Reading works of fiction can have a worldview-opening, mind-expanding effect.

3. **Exercise.** There is no better way to get blood flowing, brain cells working in overdrive, and energy levels up—all of which contributes to a greater propensity to think critically and to learn. Don't be surprised if you end up having some of your best ideas or brainstorms during your daily exercise sessions!

4. **Watch educational videos.** Do you spend your lunch hour at your desk watching YouTube videos of cats or

late-night comedians? Try using that time more productively, checking out TED talks, educational videos, or training materials from Kahn Academy or ACES!

5. **Record what you learn.** Start writing a journal—it doesn't have to be anything as public or as formal as a blog. Just jot down what you learn, think about, or create each day. Note your ideas, the skills you want to develop, interesting facts you came across—whatever. The act of writing these things down will help them stick.

You *can* grow your mind. You *can* grow your knowledge. It's worth doing, and it all begins with some simple daily habits. Like I say, "The more you know the more you grow!"

Next up, as a leader, whenever we work with people who hail from diverse backgrounds we must learn how to handle conflict!

Chapter 12

HOW TO HANDLE
CONFLICT

Conflict is Never Fun, But it is Essential.

If you're like most of the leaders I've met, one of your least favorite parts of the job is diffusing workplace conflicts. That conflicts would arise is, of course, inevitable; when people are working together in close proximity, tensions are going to develop, misunderstandings are going to happen, and feelings are going to get hurt.

Dealing with these conflicts is never fun, but it is essential—and if you do it right, you can address conflicts in a way that actually makes your team stronger.

Let me show you what I mean. What follows are a few aspects of group dynamics that every leader should keep in mind with regard to the conflict resolution process.

 Conflict is a sign that people care. Trust me, as much as you might think you want a conflict-free workplace, you don't. Not really. A workplace with no conflict is one where the team members no longer feel any enthusiasm for one another, nor any connection to their job. Conflict implies caring, and that's something you can build on.

 Conflict can be healthy. You don't want employees yelling at each other and calling one another names, but you should seek some healthy communication— and conflict can often be a catalyst for that. If you can get both people to speak directly and listen closely to one another, a conflict may actually lead to stronger bonds of teamwork.

 Conflict can often require a level-headed moderator. If you're going to try to manage the conflict, make sure you allow yourself time to cool off first. Don't let angry emotions guide your attempts at peacemaking, because it will be highly counterproductive!

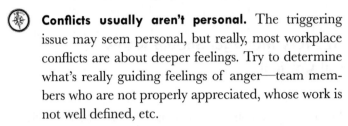 **Conflicts usually aren't personal.** The triggering issue may seem personal, but really, most workplace conflicts are about deeper feelings. Try to determine what's really guiding feelings of anger—team members who are not properly appreciated, whose work is not well defined, etc.

Conflict is best addressed through listening. Trying to stifle the feelings of your team members is dead wrong. Always give them room to vent and to explain what's really bothering them. Sometimes that can be healing in and of itself.

These principles may be useful to you as you consider the role of conflict in your workplace. Conflict can be good and improve a team's performance.

Conflict Is Good to Develop Rock Stars

As a solutions-oriented leader, you want your workplace team to run like a well-oiled machine—but when conflict rears its ugly head, your machine breaks down and your team stops working productively. For managers and HR professionals, then, resolving the conflict and moving back into a collaborative, efficient work environment is essential—but never easy!

I meet a lot of leaders who dread conflict resolution more than any other part of their work. I understand why—but here's the thing, conflict is bound to happen when you have passionate people working together under the same roof. And the sooner you come to terms with that fact, the better you'll be able to arrive at a peaceful resolution.

What Every Manager Should Know About Conflict

With that said, consider a few basic truths about conflict in the workplace:

Conflict is inevitable. Again, conflict will happen. Don't beat yourself up about it. Don't assign blame. Don't fret that you have a bad work environment. Just understand that conflict happens—and *deal with it.*

Conflict is unavoidable. Or at least it *should be.* You can try to turn a blind eye to conflict in your workspace, but then the underlying issues will fester, morale will plummet, and, most critically, your employees will lose respect for you.

Conflict is productive. Conflict is not always a bad thing. In fact, it's often an important way for employees to work out their differences and arrive at a new level of understanding with one another. So long as you facilitate conflict in a way that's solutions-driven and constructive, there's no reason why conflict can't result in positive changes.

Conflict is volatile. Of course, keeping things solutions-driven and constructive is easier said than done, as conflict can cause everyone to get a little hotheaded—but as a manager or HR employee, you have to stay above the fray. Remember, you are *management*. You're a *leader*. Your role is to facilitate, not to get sucked in.

 Conflict is unwinnable. The point is not necessarily to determine who's right and who's wrong. Conflict resolution is about letting everyone feel heard, and then providing a sense of closure—a place from which everyone feels comfortable moving forward.

None of this is meant to suggest that conflict in the workplace is fun, or that there isn't such a thing as too much of it—but when the occasional conflict arises, and you address it wisely, it can actually be a healthy thing for your team. In order to deal with conflict effectively it's important to understand what causes conflict.

What Causes Conflict?

A productive team is a unified team—a team in which all the members can cooperate and collaborate, despite any personal differences or personality clashes they may have. And to be sure, there's no such thing as a team that doesn't experience a little tension every now and again. What matters is that this tension never boils over into full-fledged, productivity-halting *conflict*.

As a leader, it's your job to minimize conflict and deal with it quickly. How can that be done? The critical first step is simply noting what tends to make conflict erupt in the first place.

What causes conflict? The answer can vary a bit from one team to the next, depending on the personalities represented and the nature of the work environment. With that said, there are a few big, conflict-causing culprits in many workplaces, including:

Miscommunication. Are you clearly conveying expectations to all of your team members—and allowing them the platform they need to communicate their feedback, their questions, and their suggestions for improvement?

Poorly defined roles. A good leader goes beyond the job description—but nevertheless, it's helpful when your team members have a clear understanding of their place within the organization and of the roles held by their peers.

Lack of goals. Are you all working toward the same end, or are there different goals in everyone's mind? Without clear, explicit goals, it's difficult to work together in a unified manner.

Lack of feedback. Do you give your team members the gift of your feedback? Without some form of feedback, team members may feel unsure of their standing in the company.

Bad company culture. Does your company run on collaboration, or does your management style pit employees against one another? A little competition is alright, but a cutthroat environment does not lend itself well to teamwork.

Personality differences. All of your team members are unique individuals, which can lead to tension; as a leader, your job is to understand these personality types and to facilitate understanding.

Remember, conflict can disrupt an otherwise productive team; understanding the root cause is the first step toward preventing it!

Conflict that is left to simmer and produce constant friction can also lead to workplace burnout affecting productivity, performance, and the happiness quotient.

The High Cost of Workplace Burnout

Let me ask you a few questions, do you have an interest in keeping workplace morale high? In protecting your employees from burnout, stress, and fatigue? In providing them with the resources they need to tackle major anxieties or seasons of struggle? Of encouraging all employees—yourself included—to take vacation time in order to recharge those batteries and stave off exhaustion?

You should and not just because it's the right thing to do. It's also something that can impact your business at the bottom line. And if you aren't mindful of workplace burnout, it could cost you big time.

Workplace Burnout Costs Businesses

Indeed, workplace burnout has become an epidemic. And as more and more leaders and employees are succumbing to the physical and emotional ravages of workplace anxiety, it costs businesses *billions* of dollars each year.

That's right, billions. And that number encompasses all of the following:

 The cost of replacing employees who leave the company because they feel overworked and underappreciated.

- The cost of sick days, call-outs, and employee absenteeism.

- Missed opportunities from sapped creativity and impaired ingenuity.

- Higher healthcare costs for your employees, which can put a big ding into workplace insurance costs.

- A general lack of energy and forward momentum.

Managing Burnout

The bottom line is that when you and your employees feel consistently burned out—beaten down by the stresses of daily life and work—it can negatively impact the entire team. So, what can be done about it?

Consider investing in stress management training, or at the very least in exemplifying stress mitigation techniques for your employees. Even communication and regular affirmation can help avert workplace burnout; hard work is easier to swallow when it seems like it's appreciated and meaningful!

Whatever you do, don't ignore the problem of burnout. If you don't deal with it early on, it could cost you *big time*.

Conclusion

CELEBRATE

SUCCESS!

Every Now and Then
Take Time to Celebrate!

What's the purpose of working hard and achieving goals if you aren't celebrating your success? The journey you started is ongoing but every now and then take time to celebrate!

Here are three ideas for celebrating victories along the road to leading a successful business. Celebrate like a rock star!

1 **Off-Campus Team Celebration:** I have found the best way to bond and celebrate with my team is to take them off campus. Getting them away from the office environment makes the celebration more special!

2 **Monthly Awards:** Monthly awards and recognition at team meetings stimulate success. When we recognize achievements in public, many times it stimulates other employees to want the same accolades, thus causing them to work harder to be the person receiving the award next month.

3 **Celebrate with a Newsletter:** Everyone loves to be named in the newspaper or seen on TV or on the company website. If you have ever been recognized publicly on television, in the newspaper, or on the web, you know what I mean. Your employees will love it and they will share the news with friends and family—it's the ultimate celebration!

When I started on my journey of discovery after failing in the early years of my professional career, I found that the principles shared throughout this book changed my life and I know each one will change your life also.

I believe with all my heart that if you follow these proven-successful principles, you will never fail like I did, and you will begin to develop your own team of leaders today!

I wish you all the success in your journey!

The Solutions-Oriented Leader Assessment

I want to thank you for taking the first step towards achieving world class results in your business and your life!

Take this complimentary Solutions-Oriented Leader Assessment and find out how you can achieve world-class results starting today!

www.rickgoodman.com/solutions-oriented-leader-assessment/

INDEX

ABOUT THE AUTHOR

The Speaker

Dr. Rick Goodman, CSP, is renowned as one of the most sought-after leadership and engagement experts in the world today. His keynote presentations and breakout sessions have produced transformational results leading to engaged employees, increased productivity and, most importantly, HIGHER PROFITS.

Dr. Rick has the distinction of delivering over 1,000 presentations in all 50 states and 16 countries. He earned the Certified Speaking Professional (CSP) designation which is the speaker profession's international measure of speaking experience and skill. Fewer than one percent of all professional speakers worldwide hold this designation.

The Author

In addition to his 30-year speaking career, Dr. Rick is the author of three books: *Living a Championship Life – A Game Plan for Success,* a book combining his success philosophy with stories compiled during his tenure as one of the team physicians for the Super Bowl champion St. Louis Rams and the St. Louis Ambush professional indoor soccer team; *My Team Sucked: Ten Rules That Turned Them Into Rock Star— A Small Book with Big Solutions* on leadership, engagement and business growth; and his latest book *The Solutions-Oriented Leader: Your Comprehensive Guide to Achieve World-Class Results.*

Dr. Rick's writing style integrates real-life stories with innovative and engaging solutions to real-world challenges. His articles are a favorite with national publications and corporate/association newsletters. His books, CDs, DVDs, online learning and virtual presentations are all designed for achievers who want to grow and implement a system that fosters great leadership!

The Entrepreneur

Dr. Rick is a successful entrepreneur who walks his talk and shares his winning philosophy with his audiences. In 1988, he created and sold one of the largest medical practices in Missouri. That same year, Dr. Rick founded a new enterprise that is still active today. His goal is to introduce his leadership and team-building formulas and systems into 10,000 businesses worldwide.

In March 2000, Dr. Rick became Vice President of Neurology Associates Group, and, in just three years, grew the franchise from two facilities to 13, with more than 100 employees and revenues in the millions. Then, in 2002, Dr. Rick also founded Advantage Continuing Education Seminars (ACES), which has become one of the fastest-growing continuing education companies in its field, providing programs in seven distinct categories, including legal, accounting, human resources, medical, construction, sales and marketing, and customer service.

The Person

Dr. Rick was born and raised in Long Island, New York, and has lived in South Florida since 2000. He attended and played ice hockey at Kent State University and received his Chiropractic degree from Logan University. He is a food and travel enthusiast. However, he will quickly tell anyone, *"I'm a citizen and student of the world!"* A proud father of Alex and Jamie, Dr. Rick stays connected with friends and people he meets around the globe as proven by his Facebook page! "I believe that the key to an awesome life is connecting and engaging in lifelong relationships!" Check him out!

For more information on Rick's speaking programs, audio programs, and learning programs, call 888-267-6098 or e-mail Rick@rickgoodman.com, or visit www.rickgoodman.com.

Follow on Twitter: https://twitter.com/DrRickGoodman

Like on Facebook: https://www.facebook.com/drrickgoodman/

Connect on LinkedIn: https://www.linkedin.com/in/drrickgoodman/

Watch on YouTube: https://www.youtube.com/c/RickGoodman

Follow on Instagram: @dr.RickGoodman